concilium

WHY THEOLOGY?

Edited by

Claude Geffré and
Werner Jeanrond

SCM Press · London

Orbis Books · Maryknoll

Published by SCM Press Ltd, 26–30 Tottenham Road, London N1
and by Orbis Books, Maryknoll, NY 10545

ISBN: 0 334 03029 3 (UK)
ISBN: 0 88344 881 5 (USA)

Typeset at The Spartan Press Ltd, Lymington, Hants
Printed by Mackays of Chatham, Kent

Concilium: Published February, April, June, August, October, December.

Contents

Introduction

Why Theology? How Theologians Today Understand Their Work

An honest report on the situation of academic theology at the end of the twentieth century will have to concede that it no longer enjoys the standing of the church, society and university that it did a few years ago. What has happened? Why is theology nowadays no longer accepted in many places as the necessary critical reflection of Christian faith upon itself, or as a significant academic discipline in the university? Why are more and more theological institutions turning into establishments for religious studies? Is theology as a critical and self-critical discussion of Christian faith now *passé*?

There are many reasons for the crisis in theology. In the West, of course, they have to do with the decline in the recognition of Christian belief. But in addition, for some Christians today belief in God is primarily synonymous with a summons to act in solidarity with the poor and oppressed of today's world. The need for critical reflection on this belief and its practical demands is all too often dismissed as superfluous, and this can very rapidly lead to a new blindness and self-righteousness.

For many church functionaries, and not just in the Roman Catholic church, theology and the criticism of the church which is associated with it is, by its very nature, quite simply a scandal. So time and again the Curia attacks 'rebellious' theologians and vice versa. The attitude of some church governments to critical theology is still not sufficiently enlightened. This situation then easily leads to a public misunderstanding of what theological thought is capable of achieving. If even their own church governments do not take theologians seriously, one can hardly expect heightened interest in theology from a public which is increasingly uninterested in the church.

But from the beginning of the Enlightenment Christian theology as an academic discipline has also time and again had to fight with the constantly changing intellectual currents in Western cultures. Can it still make a valid claim to truth, and if it can, what claim is this? Furthermore in Africa and Asia, and increasingly also in the West, Christianity is also in daily encounter with non-Christian religions. How is Christian theology to learn to understand itself in the face of a challenge from a non-Christian religious praxis and its intellectual movements?

In short, theology is involved in a learning process which makes demands from all sides on those doing theology today.

So in this issue we do not want to offer any defence of traditional theologies, but to attempt a report on the situation of theological thought in the face of these new challenges. How does theology understand itself today? What are its tasks, programmes, methods? What can theology achieve today? Who is served by theological thought? What role does theology play for Christian faith and in the quest for human truth today?

The contributions to this issue cover three areas. The first group sets out to shed more light on the current situation in theology. James Byrne points to the pluralism of contemporary theology. The quest for the one true theology or theological method is over. Today theology is a pluralistic business. A unitary theology is no longer being forced on all the corners of the world, but there is an increasing readiness for theological discussion with particular contexts of theology. The rise of regional or even local theologies is certainly enriching the theological cosmos, but it confronts all those engaged in theological thinking in different contexts with the heightened need for a dialogue between their different theologies. A new readiness to discuss with those of different theological views is required today of all theologians.

Roger Haight similarly investigates this new starting point for theological thought and notes that this change of context for theology is of course also accompanied by a change in the responsibility of the individual theologian. Whereas theologians were formerly responsible only confessionally, to their own churches, in our ecumenical age they have to give an account of themselves to several communities within the Christian movement at the same time. The many shifts of theological awareness also include a heightened recognition of the social nature of human beings and the needs which arise from this.

From an empirical perspective, Carl Reinhold Bråkenhielm offers a case-study of religious self-understanding in Sweden, the first post-Christian land in the Western hemisphere. He warns theologians to be careful in any theological interpretation of local factors and to look more closely at the actual situation of our societies before engaging in attempts at theological correlation between Christian symbols and present-day cultures.

Four questions of the contemporary theological programme are discussed in the second part of this issue: the question of God, the eschatological character of Christian faith, the question of truth in the face of religious pluralism and the problem of universal theological thought-patterns.

David Tracy welcomes the rekindling of interest in God in our postmodern age. This new interest is not in the traditional ontological approach to God but in the surprising presence of God in our world which cannot be domesticated or controlled. The God who is love can only be thought of constantly anew as a gracious, loving, good God beyond all speculation on being, beyond our rationality and ideas of relationship. Postmodern approaches can accordingly prove surprising allies on the way to a new openness to the biblical experience of God.

In this connection Nicholas Lash investigates the conditions under which Christian eschatology can be articulated today. The challenge for Christianity consists in recognizing absolute finality without accepting institutional forms and mental attitudes which seek to derive authoritarian capital from the eschatological character of Christian faith.

With regard to the pluralistic context of theological thought, John Thiel endorses the revaluation of regional truth-claims in theology. Such regional truth-claims, which of course always already presuppose universal truth-claims, must first prove their authority in dialogue with other truth-claims. But they are the best guarantee that human experience with its particular characteristics will be taken seriously in theology. Accordingly, the Christian tradition can be understood as a network of regional and universal truth-claims related to one another.

Aloysius Pieris takes this notion further in connection with the problem of inculturation. He discusses different theological models, all of which originally come from a particular culture, and shows how one model indebted to particular philosophical interests, the *logos* model, has become the universal model of the Western sphere of culture. However, today it is important to rehabilitate forgotten or suppressed theological thought-models (the *dabar* model and the *hodos* model) and investigate their potential to lead to a more holistic type of thinking in theology.

The contemporary discussion of method in theology is demonstrated by means of three examples. First Klaus Berger (an exegete) and José Alemany (a systematic theologian) discuss the relationship between exegesis and systematic theology. Here Berger emphasizes that the dialogue between the two cannot succeed as long as the exegete is unwilling to take into account the connection between exegesis and systematic theology and the systematic theologian is unwilling to take into account the connection between systematic theology and exegesis. Here too there is an indication of better, more thoroughly thought out, collaboration within theology since, as Alemany emphatically confirms, both exegete and systematic theologian are both finally obligated to the elucidation of the truth of Christian faith.

In her contribution, Anne Fortin-Melkevik discusses the range of interdisciplinary work in present-day theology. For her there is no doubt that theology needs to be done in interdisciplinary discussion. She goes further, and emphasizes the degree to which once-cherished presuppositions in theology must now be rethought in dialogue with other disciplines (social sciences, humanities, hermeneutics, and so on). So interdisciplinary work is not an end in itself, but a characteristic of theological thought which must react appropriately today to the challenges both within it and outside it.

Finally, Norbert Mette investigates the effects of these new reflections about theology on the study of theology itself. He indicates the differing horizons which exist between the institutional church's attempts to order the conception and organization of theological study on the one hand and the expectations of the students themselves on the other. Here more appropriate pedagogical and didactic reflection is urgently needed on the whole of theology.

Thus the contributions in this issue attempt from their very different horizons of experience and perspectives to offer a dynamic picture of theological thinking. On the one hand, today Christian theology understands itself more than ever in a global context; on the other hand, it is more than ever before attempting to enter into regional and local experiences of faith and the church so as to do justice to its task of providing appropriate reflection on Christian faith and the service to the church which is associated with it. It has become more interdisciplinary, and is increasingly liberating itself from the traditionally monistic compulsions of its quest for methods. So Christian theology has certainly become much more complicated; however, as this issue seeks to document, it also speaks with many more voices and has become more exciting.

Claude Geffré
Werner Jeanrond

I · The Situation

Theology and Christian Faith

James M. Byrne

In the tradition of Western Christianity, theology has been generally considered as a second-order reflection on the first order of Christian faith. However, this formal distinction brings with it certain difficulties: these include the fact that the faith that is believed (*fides quae*) is itself partly the product of theological reflection; the blurring of the distinction in a situation where theology itself constitutes part of the activity of believing (as in the contemporary experience of some basic Christian communities); and the question as to whether this distinction is an idealist construct. These caveats notwithstanding, however, it seems useful to continue to identify theology as a secondary reflection on the fundamental experience of being Christian in the world, for theology *in se* cannot be identified with Christian faith, even though Christian faith is always expressed in the form of a theology; i.e. doctrines, Christian anthropology, liturgical prayers, etc. are always formulated in the language of theology and their formulation is open to theological critique.

What do we mean by 'Christian faith'? Christian faith is constituted by both the subjective activity of believing and the content of what is believed (the *fides qua* and the *fides quae*). Christian faith is an affirmative response, a 'Yes' to life, not on account of some abstract principle but on account of the particularity of Jesus Christ.[1] Of course this 'Yes' to Jesus Christ and to the God revealed by him often entails a 'No' to many aspects of a broken and unjust reality. I shall therefore use the term 'Christian faith' as a unifying term to refer to a dipolar reality with subjective and objective content. The fact that these poles are not static and are open to modulation both in themselves and in their relations makes the activity we call 'theology' possible.

This much granted, I shall examine the topic of theology and Christian faith in four sections: 1. The historical background to contemporary theology; 2. Formal distinctions in theology; 3. Difficulties for contemporary theology; 4. Theology in the service of Christian faith.

I The historical background to contemporary theology

To understand the context of contemporary theology it is useful to look briefly at the major theological developments in this century. The early part of the century saw controversy in both Catholic and Protestant theology. The Catholic controversy centred on the Modernist movement and its protagonists Tyrrell and Loisy. The suppression of Modernism by Pius X set the tone for the tension between the Roman magisterium and theologians who see the need for an ongoing *aggiornamento* to meet the demands of the modern world; periods of theological *aggiornamento* are usually followed by periods of regression. After the suppression of the Modernists there followed a period of entrenchment which was disturbed by the emergence of the *nouvelle théologie* in the 1940s and 1950s; despite the attempts to silence individual theologians, this theology emerged triumphant at Vatican II, showing that the neo-scholastic theology and the mediaeval view of Christianity which had dominated the church since Trent was inadequate to meet the demands of the modern world. After Vatican II there was an explosion of theological activity, renewed ecumenism and the growth of liberation theology. However, this promising beginning did not develop as it could have due to the continued attempts by Rome to control theologians. In the context of the whole church we are now in a period of regression.

Other factors of importance in the course of this century include the acceptance of critical biblical scholarship, the development of the church's social teaching, and the controversies over sexual ethics.

Protestant theology began the century dominated by the influence of nineteenth-century liberalism, but was suddenly shocked by the publication of Karl Barth's *Römerbrief*, which rejected the dominant consensus. Since then Protestant theology has operated within the polarities of Barth on the one hand and the demythologized Christian existentialism of Rudolf Bultmann on the other. Bultmann's demythologization programme was taken to its extreme limit in the 1960s by the 'death of God' theology, but at its best it remains part of the mainstream of both Protestant and Catholic thinking. The narrative emphasis in Barth's theology has recently been given new impetus by the development by the Yale School in the United States of a 'post-liberal' theology which rejects many of the assumptions of the dominant academic theology on the nature of human experience, in favour of a reassertion of the particularity of the Christian narrative. Other important factors in Protestant theology in this century have been the emergence of a 'social gospel' theology and the recent moves in the Anglican Communion towards the ordination of women; there has also been an increased concern with issues of justice in many churches, particularly among Methodists.

In summary, theology at the end of the twentieth century is marked by an inescapable pluralism that provides a great richness, but also presents some obvious difficulties in reaching theological agreement.

II Formal distinctions in theology

Because of the plurality of contemporary theologies it is impossible to give a general description of theology; however, we can make some distinctions on the formal level which may be helpful in relating theology to Christian faith.

I shall distinguish two formal levels of theology. The first level is the recognition that central to the nature of humanity is reflection on the meaning of life in the context of the totality of creation; from this first level emerge inescapably the question of God and the question of the value and purpose of human life in the world. At this primary level of reflection, theology arises alongside other forms of rationality such as logic. While some Protestant theologians may be suspicious of this level of theology (rejecting it as merely human activity), there is no doubting the existence of such human thinking. This first level of theology has been interpreted in the Catholic tradition as a form of a natural theology, and it has been brought to prominence in the twentieth century in the transcendental theology of Rahner, de Lubac *et al.* This is essentially an understanding of theology as reflection upon experience, and it requires no professional training in theological disciplines.

The second level is the definition of theology as a science, carried on primarily in the university or academy. The scientific nature of theology was outlined classically by Aquinas in the thirteenth century. However, it has not always enjoyed a pre-eminent position among Christians: it has been criticized implicitly by alternative forms of mystical theology (e.g. Eckhart, the radical Reformers) and Christian activism (e.g. the Franciscans, Pietism), and explicitly on grounds of experience (Luther), liberation (which accuses it of ideological links with the capitalist economic structure) and authority (which resents its freedom). More recently, the status of theology as a discipline worthy of the epithet 'scientific' has come under attack in the nineteenth and twentieth centuries by scientific and linguistic positivism in various forms.

I believe that these formal distinctions are important for the current situation of theology because with the development of the human sciences (anthropology, psychology, sociology, etc.) theology has been given the tools with which the second level of scientific reflection may interpret the first level of human experience and praxis. This accounts both for the critical task of reinterpreting the Christian faith which theology undertakes in changing situations, and for the interest which theology shares with other disciplines which investigate the human condition. One of the major points of difference between a critical theology and a reactionary theology is the extent to which conclusions drawn from the diversity of human experience and reached with the aid of other disciplines should be regarded as normative theological criteria.

III Difficulties for contemporary theology

Before an outline of some of the difficulties for contemporary theology, two important aspects of the contemporary context must be acknowledged. These are the emergence of many different theologies all over the world, and the problematic status of traditional academic theology.

The first aspect is that the emergence of 'local' theologies has led to the recognition of the importance of discrete experiences in theological reflection. By 'local' here I mean both the ethnic theologies which emerged in the meeting of the faith with local culture (as in South-East Asia and Africa) and theologies which grew from particular experiences, but which have more general significance (as in the well-known liberation and feminist theologies). Many of these 'local' theologies have been critical of what they considered to be an academically-centred and male-dominated North Atlantic theology which did not do justice to the multiplicity of cultures and experiences. These theologies have achieved some success in making theology relevant to the life of Christian communities precisely by the way in which they correlate the gospel with concrete local experiences, and draw on those experiences as a way of responding anew to the gospel. Many of these theologies tend to assume the methodological priority of criteria drawn from the cultural or political experience of particular groups (e.g. criteria such as the cultural imperialism of Western theology, the fundamental option for the poor, the structural injustice of patriarchy).

The second aspect relates to 'scientific' academic theology. It is widely believed that this form of theology is in decline, especially in the Western university context. Now if comparison is made with the central role of theology in the mediaeval university this is certainly true, but such a comparison is spurious. What is not in doubt, however, is that theology no longer enjoys any privileged status *vis-à-vis* other disciplines. Here a multitude of historical, philosophical, cultural and political factors must be taken into account, factors which in effect amount to the history of the secularization of Western society. Lamenting this history is pointless; what is required is an analysis of the contemporary factors over which theology and theologians have some influence in order to keep a critical and creative academic theology at the service of the whole Christian community and as a strong voice in society. However, this task is made more difficult by the fact that academic theology has to cope not only with a secularized society and a frequent anti-religious bias in the university, but also with attacks from religious authorities, who have also not hesitated to attack some 'local' theologies.

Thus, the present situation of theology is paradoxical in so far as an increase in theological reflection at the local level exists alongside, and has been partly based upon, an apparent weakening in the status of classical academic theology. There is a further paradox in the situation of academic theology, which has seen increased activity yet seems to be marginalised *vis-à-vis* the power structures of the church, especially in Roman Catholicism.

One thing that is certain, however, is that it is almost impossible to speak of 'theology' as if there were one unified discourse which could be identified and manipulated for better or worse: this is the illusion and the hope held by reactionary conservatives and transcendental idealists alike, but the reality of cultural and theological pluralism rules this out. The fact of this inescapable plurality enormously complicates the task of analysing the relationship of theology and Christian faith, for it must be made clear which theology is at work and in what context the discourse is taking place: the hope for a general theology (or even a 'Universal' Catechism) would appear to be both foolish and arrogant. It would be equally unwise to attempt to delineate what the relationship between theology and Christian faith *should* be at the present time, for in a pluralist situation that will depend upon the specific ecclesial and political conditions. I shall therefore outline only some formal difficulties for contemporary theology, before making some suggestions as to how theology can maintain its essential critical and constructive function in the Christian community.

(a) Some difficulties external to theology
(i) Since the the Enlightenment there has been an increased lack of confidence in all non-scientific cognitive claims. A tradition of systematic doubt runs through European thought from Descartes, Hume and Kant to nineteenth-century positivism and twentieth-century analytic philosophy. A 'hard' epistemology of the natural sciences has come to dominate a 'soft' epistemology of the human sciences; this division has taken root in the

popular mind, to the detriment of religion. Theology must respond critically to scientific or popular forms of rationalism which caricature 'non-scientific' thinking as meaningless; but it must also reaffirm that a critical rationality is compatible with both modern science and with faith. Indeed, one of the most important roles which theology can play in relation to the faith of the Christian community is to criticize the dualism which sometimes separates faith and reason, belief and science. A constructive theology will reaffirm that a mature faith requires a critical rationality but need not be destroyed by it. This is one of the premises on which modern theology finds its rationale, but it is not always evident to believers.

(ii) Moral discourse has become incommensurate. By this I mean that any hope for a unified context of public discourse, which to some extent characterized mediaeval thought (although we now know that there was more plurality than had been previously acknowledged) and which the rationalism of the Enlightenment hoped would banish all obscurantism, has retreated in the face of a plurality of discourses. Ethical and political problems such as wealth distribution, abortion, the status of women and homosexuals in church and society appear to be marked by differences so great that there often seems to be no common ground on which different views can be reconciled and solutions reached. In this situation of *de facto* relativism, theology has no privileged position. Social and legal changes in many matters of ethical importance are achieved more often by effective lobbying of politicians and officials than by the form of rational discourse in which theology has traditionally engaged.

In such a situation theological thinking must finally recognize that it is no longer possible to deduce specific moral or doctrinal norms from general theories of natural law or revelation in scripture, and then fit experience into the pre-determined moral framework. It is this essentially mediaeval world-view which has led to the situation in Roman Catholicism where the official teaching on contraception is repeated *ad nauseam*, even though it is widely ignored, and in Anglicanism to the division generated by the question of the ordination of women to the priesthood. In this situation a theology which can balance the received tradition with valid theological criteria based on human experience is essential (e.g. the experience of women as a criterion in ecclesiology and the theology of ministry; the experience of the marginalized in developing church social teaching; the experience of the laity in sexual ethics). Such a theology can play an important mediating role between the tradition and the contemporary experience of the Christian community, and by so doing can begin to bring the shared ethical reflection of the Christian community into the wider society.

Theology can make a specific Christian contribution, however, only if it keeps the 'otherness' generated by the plurality of experience to the forefront of theological awareness. Theodor Adorno once remarked that those in power see as human only their own reflected image, instead of reflecting the human as that which is precisely different.[2] A theology which is not a theology of the 'other' can easily become simply a rationalization for oppression, particularly when that theology operates from a position of power.

(iii) The third point follows from this. It is well known that many theologians, catechists, workers for justice and others suffer persecution at the hands of religious authorities for not professing the 'correct' theology – while cases such as those of Leonardo Boff and Hans Küng have received much attention, this persecution also goes on at a local diocesan and even parish level. This is not simply an issue of competing intellectual interpretations of the Christian faith. It is often a question of something as fundamental as how to follow Christ in a particular situation, of when to speak and when to act; in many parts of the world it is often a matter of life and death, and is thus at the very heart of faith. However, oppression does not always cause revolution; in a voluntary organization such as the church it can also cause indifference. Commenting on the sexual teaching of John Paul II, Jacques Pohier observes 'the way in which the very spectacular action of this very spectacular pope meets with such obvious failure in this sphere that he does not even provoke the slightest discussion and disturbance among the believers who are so interested in him'.[3] The possibility of theological reflection involving the faith-experience of Christian men and women can be destroyed by despair and indifference.

(b) Difficulties internal to theology

(i) Regarding the Christian tradition, critical historical thinking has not had the effect it could have had. Despite successful investigation into the tradition on important practical matters such as church collusion with oppression, sexuality, the status of women, etc., many believers continue to hold the myth that the content of church teaching has remained unchanged for ever. The ongoing development of a critical and practical hermeneutical theology is one area where 'local' and 'academic' theologies can work effectively together, so that the knowledge gained from theological investigation can have an effect in practical matters. There are a number of areas of practical concern where progress must still be made against ahistorical interpretations of the Christian faith; these include the question of the development of the theology of ministry, inter-church marriage, shared eucharist with other Christian churches, the status of the divorced and remarried, and the participation of the laity in church government.

(ii) There is also uncertainty in academic theology about the status of experience as a theological criterion. The influential analysis of the transcendental horizon of the basic experience of being human made by Rahner and others in mid-century has been overtaken by a pluralist situation in which different experiences are given hermeneutical priority by different groups of theologians (the best known being the 'preferential option for the poor' of liberation theology). Depending on which experience is given priority, a different theological emphasis emerges. The difficulty of this state of affairs (which as a methodological problem is common to all Christian theology) has been compounded in Catholicism by increasing attempts by Rome to integrate specific moral teachings (especially *Humanae Vitae*) into the core of the faith. This attempt at forced agreement by means of an ontology of belief to solve open problems in epistemology or ethics not only does violence to theology and to the tradition but is also philosophically absurd. Immeasurable damage is caused both to the Christian community and to the faith of believers when the authorities of the church ignore the *sensus fidelium* in favour of a 'gradual infallibility' in sexual ethics and other areas. In a situation of theological and cultural plurality a critical and constructive theology will continue to assert the value of the *sensus fidelium*, the experience of the Christian community, not only as an abstract theological principle but as a criterion of theological judgment in specific circumstances.

(iii) The separation of the theological disciplines continues to cause difficulties. The reason for this separation are complex, but have more to do with the division of labour in the university than with the needs of ordinary Christians. Much of what is called systematic theology continues to operate within the framework of German idealism, which largely isolates it from scripture and ethics. Enormous achievements have been made in biblical scholarship, but I think that it is true to say that the theological conclusion which most theologians have drawn from the use of the historical-critical method (i.e. that revelation is historically dependent and mediated) does not yet form part of the horizon of faith of the Christian community as a whole.

Theology includes biblical interpretation, and today this interpretation takes place in a context of pluralism. In this pluralistic context fixed interpretations are challenged, but there is also a challenge to the traditional divisions of the theological disciplines. One locus of Christian life where systematic theology and scriptural scholarship can meet creatively is in the preaching, catechetics and theological reflection of the local community; and in the context of the local community fresh interpretations, even from outside the Christian community (as in the work of writers, artists and film-makers), can be brought to bear on the traditional texts. As J. Severino Croatto points out, critical interpretation of scripture 'is also practised *from within a particular* (social or theological) *locus* – that is, from within a given (pre)conception of reality. Hence all *exegesis* is also *eisegesis*.'[4] In the attempt of the local Christian community to discern God's revelation here and now we can see that Scripture teaches us not that it is the end of revelation, but rather part of ongoing revelation; as Croatto emphasizes, Scripture ' . . . teaching us, precisely, to recognize God *in present self-revelations*, and not as a repetition of the past'.[5] An integrated theology is one which does not keep Christian life or theological reflection compartmentalized along the lines of the university faculty, but instead believes that God's Spirit can work an ongoing revelation in the theological activity of each local church.

IV Theology in the service of Christian faith

The majority of Christian believers have no direct contact with the practice of formal theology, yet they all possess a theology – that is, some rudimentary ideas about the things they believe. They all have a concept of God, some idea of what Jesus did and said, a basic understanding of the relationship between love of neighbour and salvation; unfortunately, they may also believe that members of other faiths are damned, that Jesus was not truly human, that religious relics work magic or that salvation consists in repeating the literal words of the Bible. Changes to an erroneous theology or belief can be effected by means of the mediation of a critically improved theology (as in post-Vatican II Catholicism). As I have said, however, positive change can also be mediated in the other direction when the experience of faith calls the standard theology into question (as in the Reformation and some recent 'local' theologies). Both these processes require the mediation of the trained theologian (not necessarily the university professor, but also the informed teacher, the lay leader, catechist, or minister). Thus, in the most practical terms, Christian faith requires the ongoing presence of well-trained and knowledgable theologians.

The role of theology in the Christian community is essentially this role of critical mediation between the Christian faith as it is handed down in the tradition and the contemporary living experience of Christians. It is the hermeneutical task of a twofold interpretation. As an interpretative activity, theology is not tied to the preservation of faith in a particular format; nor is it free to destroy the faith that is there in the Christian community. Its task is rather the critical preservation of both; it is a task of service. But this service is not undertaken for the sake of theology or theologians; just as Christian faith, properly understood, finds its true end in love and justice, so too theology is at the service of Christian praxis in the world. In this century we have learned from ideology-critique that ideas are not innocent, and cannot be separated without cost from their social, political or ecclesial context. Thus, the requirement which Christian faith makes of theology and its praxis is the requirement integral to Christian faith itself, namely that it should be not only an agent of understanding but also an agent of transformation.

Notes

1. See Theodor Schneider, *Was Wir Glauben*, Düsseldorf 1985, 26.
2. Theodor Adorno, *Minima Moralia: Reflections from Damaged Life*, London 1974, 68.
3. Jacques Pohier, *God – in Fragments*, London 1985, 179.
4. Severino Croatto, *Biblical Hermeneutics: Toward a Theory of Reading as the Production of Meaning*, Maryknoll 1987, 67.
5. Ibid., 74. See also Cristina Grenholm, 'Christian Interpretation of the Old Testament in a Pluralistic Context', *Studia Theologica* 2, 1994.

The Church as Locus of Theology

Roger Haight

The church is the home of theological reflection. The importance of theology for the church lies in the fact that theology includes reflection on the basis, goals and intrinsic ministerial operations of the church. Every organization needs ongoing critical review of its grounding vision and mission. And reciprocally, the church is important for theology as the institution dedicated to preserving and nurturing the faith in the light of which theologians speak. The church provides the living version of the faith out of which the theologian works.

This article attempts to give an account of these mutual relationships. In order to do this in the brief space provided I shall focus on some developments that have occurred in the world and in the church and how these changes have influenced the church, theology and theology in the church. Four developments have had a direct influence on the place of theology in the church today: the knowledge explosion, the ecumenical movement, inter-religious dialogue, and the rise of liberation movements. In what follows I shall simply point out how these movements have had quite a sharp impact on the inter-relationship between church and theology. But before enumerating these developments, I begin by offering a generalized descriptive definition of theology, a conception that is presupposed in this article.

Theology in the church

All are familiar with a variety of brief definitions or descriptions of theology. These are helpful at least in order to clarify the background and suppositions of the author in question. In what follows I shall work with the following understanding of the discipline of Christian theology: theology is the attempt to construe the whole of reality, the world, human existence, its history, and God, in the light of the symbols of the Christian tradition. This definition has several advantages. On the one hand it opens up the object of theology to all reality. Theology does not merely have the narrow scope of talk about God. Everything directly or indirectly comes under the scrutiny of the Christian theological imagination. But on the other hand, the formal and defining characteristic of this discipline is determined by the tradition of the religious symbols of Christianity. Scripture has a priority of place in this history, but that and the reasons for it need not be developed here.

Christian theology both emerges out of the Christian community and is directed back towards it. When looked at pragmatically, it becomes apparent that all thinking and reflection emerges out of life and life experiences. Thus theological reflection is born and nurtured within the Christian community. But this community has a tradition, and the lived experience of the community has been recorded and preserved in the history of behaviour and symbols that define its identity and language. The history of the religious symbols of the community are the primary data or witnesses for the theologians' attempts at interpreting present-day reality.

But secondly, the reflection that grows out of the life of the community should by the same pragmatic principle be directed back to this same historical and spiritual life. All knowledge is for living. Thus one of the measures of the value of a theology, beyond its faithfulness to its symbolic sources and its intelligibility, is its relevance to the actual lives of the people who make up the church and its ability to empower those lives.

Given these general parameters for theology within the church, what are some of the developments in the modern period generally, and particularly over the past decades, that have altered previous notions of theology and given it a particular bearing today?

The idea of place

One spontaneously speaks of the church as the locus or place for the unfolding of theological reflection. One does theology in the church. However, because the metaphor of 'place' is a physical and spatial image, it connotes clear boundaries. And some analyses of the distinct nature of theology as a discipline have strengthened the idea that the range of the object of theology is limited. As a first thesis I want to stress that while theology is at home in the church, its subject matter is not limited to ecclesial matters.

One of many historical developments that have encouraged a limiting conception of the church as the place of theology is the explosion of knowledge in the modern period. In archaic societies it is sometimes difficult to distinguish the boundaries between religion, social arrangement and economic life. By contrast, modern developed societies have become more complex. Within the congeries of relationships that make up contemporary life people distinguish between ways of knowing, kinds of knowledge and kinds of reality that are known. Along with an increasing number of differentiations in knowledge one also finds a tendency toward compartmentalization of separate spheres of knowledge. Theology pertains to religion; Christian theology is what is done in and for the church; theology becomes more and more sectarian. At an extreme, theology becomes incomprehensible to any one who is not an educated church member.

The localization and compartmentalization of theology is a temptation for many today. Some theologians have become seduced by the very systems of modernity and postmodernity which they attack. That is, they try to escape them by isolating the church from culture and conceiving of theology as a purely confessional and fideist discipline. Other people compartmentalize reality psychologically. They say, for example, that a particular course of action is a business decision but not an ethical decision, or an ethical decision but with no religious import. These divisions between spheres of reality are forms of blindness, or at least myopia. Formal differentiations of methods and kinds of knowledge are essential for clear, critical thinking, but they do not define separable spheres of reality. As in archaic societies the reality of human life is one, and its various facets are organically inter-related. One cannot carve out a space for theology that is unrelated to the whole sphere of human life including all of its actual physical, secular, cultural and religious dimensions.

This first thesis is against one form of Christian sectarianism. The church is the place of theology, but the church cannot and does not limit or confine theology to merely ecclesial matters. In the Roman Catholic Church, Vatican II's decree *Gaudium et spes* overcame all such sectarianism by proposing the church as an open community defined by its mission to the world. All reality is the subject-matter of theology and therefore provides data for it. Theology seeks to understand all reality through the light of Christian symbols. Besides God, the whole of the *humanum* and the *mundum* define the range and scope of theology.

The idea of church

A second development in the conception of theology in the church has been occasioned or caused by the ecumenical movement. The seeds of the ecumenical movement were sown with the nineteenth-century consciousness of historicity and it emerged formally in the twentieth century. The Roman Catholic Church at first resisted ecumenism as a sign of religious indifferentism, but with Vatican II it has committed itself to participation in the quest for Christian unity. From the earliest witness to church life in the New Testament and the Apostolic Fathers, the unity of the church has been a dominant value and theme in the church's self-understanding.

At present one could probably divide all Christian theologians into two camps: those evangelicals who reject the ecumenical movement and those who have internalized the premises upon which it rests. Conservative evangelical theologians look with suspicion on what, from the point of view of fundamentalism and naive ideas of biblical inerrancy, appears to be liberal unfaithfulness to scriptural revelation. But from the perspective of the various mainline churches of the world the church itself must be conceived universally as the one great church which is in fact institutionally divided. Seen historically in its genesis and development, and against the background of other religions, the church appears as one but fragmented. The task of ecumenism, therefore, is to give historical form to already existing reality. Within the ecumenical movement, theology that is done in the church is done ecumenically; it is a function of the great church. Theology that is purely confessional, that is, the theology of a particular church over against the great church, would be anti-ecumenical in so far as it did not take into account the existence and data of the whole church. Such a theology would not promote unity but would work against it.

The relation between ecumenical theology and that of particular churches is dialectical. The primary referent of 'the Christian church' is recognized to be the great church, the whole historical movement of Christianity. Historical consciousness and the ecumenical movement forbid *a priori* definitions of the church that exclude particular churches without making a detailed historical and doctrinal case for it. But at the same time no church theologian or ecclesiologist is a member of the church at large. Theology is done by particular theologians within a particular church. It is inevitable, then, that the historical context of the theologian provides the matrix for his or her theology. But theologians should be aware of this and consciously frame their theology in the broader perspective. Their reasoning must take other churches into account. In various degrees present-day theologians have been able to transcend the narrow confines of their own churches without being unfaithful to them; they have read and been influenced by other theologians and churches and adopted an ecumenical perspective. More and more today Christian theology is becoming an ecumenical discipline in fact without particular theologians surrendering their confessional alliances and identities.

But if these reflections on the ecumenical character of theology are accurate, then the role of the authority of any particular church relative to the theologian and his or her theology will have changed. And by extension, the role of the authority of individual churches shifts with respect to the discipline of theology itself. In an ecumenically conscious theology the witness and data of the magisterium of the particular theologian by definition ceases to be the sole point of reference for authoritative statements. Again, by extension to the discipline, ecumenical theology must consider a variety of authoritative witnesses from many churches. It must also employ various comparative and dialectical procedures to frame a more general statement of the issue than will be reflected in the particular view of only one church. Theology that is ecumenically conscious is led by a logic other than reliance on the magisterium of a single church and is forced to consult the authorities of all churches in a reverent and critical manner.

The authority structures of different churches vary in many respects. But as far as the Roman Catholic Church is concerned, its commitment to the ecumenical movement at Vatican II alters the role of the magsterium when it is directed towards theology and changes the role of theology as well. Perhaps a loose historical analogy will help to indicate the nature of the shift. Theology in the Roman Catholic Church after Vatican II's endorsement of ecumenism is roughly analogous to theology during the Western Schism (1378–1417). Catholic theologians then existed within the sphere of one of the two popes or three popes. Theoretically they were bound by the magisterium and papal authority of their particular pope. Yet most of those theologians, especially those in the university centres, knew they had a higher loyalty to the *congregatio fidelium* which was one in Christ. Here theology rose above 'local' or 'sectarian' or 'confessional' authority, was critical of it and of the situation itself, and in this transcending role helped form the atmosphere or situational climate in which a resolution was effected.

It should not be thought that the role or importance of the magisterium of any particular church is minimized by these considerations. Only exaggerated claims of the authority within any particular communion is affected. Particular structures of authority in different communions are essential for preserving the distinctive spirit of these traditions in a pluralistic church. A magisterium is absolutely necessary to define the beliefs of a particular tradition, to establish boundaries of this or that communion, to organize and regulate and thus preserve the identity of it and the people in it. What the internalization of the ecumenical imperative by the churches has done, then, is to moderate the absolutistic or universalistic claims of certain structures of authority in particular churches.

Let me summarize this point in the form of a thesis. It is directed against another form of sectarianism. The church is the place for theology. But the church at the end of the twentieth century as a result of the ecumenical movement is recognized to be the whole or total church, despite its disunity and divisions. This means, negatively, that the church in the sense of a particular communion cannot by itself be a final or exclusive limit or constraint or criterion or norm for Christian theology today. Rather, positively, the many magisteria of various churches are witnesses to Christian truth and sources for data for Christian theology.

The idea of theology

It is not my intention at this point to propose an integral concept of the sources, nature and method of theology in the church. Rather, I want simply to indicate one way in which the discipline of theology has been altered during the course of the twentieth century by inter-religious encounter.

People who have received a university education ordinarily acquire an historical consciousness. This awareness of the historically conditioned character of all human reality, of its particularity in time and place, is mediated by critical study. However, an historical consciousness can also be mediated more generally by the experience of pluralism across cultures in every domain of life, especially the most fundamental, such as family, the sphere of national and cultural values, and religion. To the extent that various forms of communication today allow people to share in a global consciousness, in the same measure they recognize that religious pluralism is simply a fact or a given. Consciousness of it is becoming more accentuated as groups migrate and carry their religions with them. More and more religious pluralism is directly visible as religions share space in cities around the world.

As the fact of religious pluralism becomes accepted, and then taken for granted, attitudes towards other religions also change. Given the transcendent mystery of God, should one not expect different religions that correlate closely with different cultures? And given the Christian conception of a God of boundless love, should one not expect God to engage all people, and thus interact with different people on their own terms? The attitudes of Christians towards other religions have changed profoundly in recent times; they view other religions more positively. And Christian theology has reflected these attitudes by a variety of explanations of how God's salvific grace is at work in them.

This development entails a new posture of the church *vis à vis* other religions and consequently a new dimension for theological reflection within the church. In very broad terms one can define the new stance of the church in terms of the categories of witness and dialogue. The mission of the church in one respect remains the same: it is a mission of evangelization or giving witness to its faith in God mediated by Jesus Christ. Its intent is to be a sign of this faith and to establish and nurture a local church to continue the mission of Jesus. But at the same time the notion of dialogue has come to inform and qualify the method and immediate goals of the witness. Dialogue means entering into a respectful and attentive exchange with people, their cultures and their religions. The metaphor of a dialogue or conversation supplies the rules for how the church should encounter the people of other religions at all levels. In other words, a phenomenology of an authentic dialogue reveals the characteristics that should qualify the unfolding of the church's mission.

What does the encounter with and consciousness of other religions and the consequent dialogical character of the church's mission imply for the nature of theology today? How do the characteristics of dialogue come to bear on theology? Much could be said here, but two points go some distance towards the essence of the matter.

First, the interiorization of historicity encourages a certain humility or modesty in the Christian witness to ultimate truth. This is not a modesty that stems from uncertainty and doubt: Christians know what they have experienced of God through Jesus Christ. But Christian experience of God is also characterized by mystery and unknowing. And Jesus is a particular, historically conditioned mediation of God. The Christian today should share a sense of the limitations and culturally conditioned character of the Christian tradition. The Christian should also be open to more and fuller dimensions of an encounter with the same God that is revealed in Jesus but also mediated through other religions.

Secondly, and correspondingly, in a situation that can be characterized as dialogical in nature, as opposed to being initially polemical, Christian theology is attentive to the voice of dialogue partners. Christian theology is open to learning. The experience of non-Christians becomes in some sense data for Christian theology. The consequences of this have been clearly described by theologians who have engaged in inter-religious dialogues: the understanding of their own faith has been changed. The dialogue, the passing over and entering into the world of the other religion, to whatever extent this is possible, and the return, transform Christian self-understanding.

This third thesis can be stated succinctly; it too is against yet another form of Christian sectarianism. The church is the place for theology. But the encounter of the church in this century with other religions has transformed the church's understanding of its mission. Theology in such a church is also transformed. On the one hand, in a dialogical situation its affirmations become more modest, less all-knowing, simpler, and more open to deepening and renewal. On the other hand, theology learns from non-Christian experience. The sources and data for Christian theology are thus further expanded beyond the Christian sphere to the worlds of religious experience in which it is in dialogue.

The focus of theology

Finally, there is another shift in theology within the church which has occurred over the past two centuries but which has been accented in the last three decades. This shift moves from a focus on human existence individually conceived to human existence both personally and socially conceived. The media of this development most recently have been the problems addressed by liberation theology, political theology, feminist theology and those particular theologies that attend to specific forms of corporate human suffering and oppression.

Modern theology is often characterized as shifting its point of departure and focus from the positive, objective data of Christian tradition and authority to religious experience. Modern theology has turned to the subject, to religious anthropology, to experience of transcendence as the basis for theological affirmation. But the social consequences of the industrial revolution which spawned the social gospel, and the increasingly global, social, political and economic problems of the twentieth century which have generated various liberation theologies qualify how the turn to the human subject is to be understood. An individualistic understanding of the human is simply inadequate: its abstraction leaves behind the real situation of the individual. The fundamental character of the shift mediated by socially conscious theologies, therefore, is anthropological. Human existence cannot be understood outside a social-historical context. The individually unique and spiritual person, when he or she is really understood existentially and concretely, is seen to be a social individual.

This new social focus of Christian theology has several consequences for theology in the church today. Of the many, two seem to be most important.

First, theology today must explicitly address the seeming meaningless-ness of human history for so many human beings. The message of hope for an external fulfilled life with God certainly does address the question of human history with the conviction that history has an ultimate aim or goal. But it is not the end of history or human life that is so problematic for so many people today. The problem is time or history itself. Evil has taken on a qualitatively new historical dimension. The increase of world population plus the advances in modern technology have resulted in shocking and scandalizing levels of mass human suffering. One must show how God's end for history bends back and influences the unfolding of history itself. The problem is serious: human experience rebels at the senselessness of the human condition that human beings have created and there does not seem to be any conceivable way to redress the suffering. Human beings have to get on with their own lives; they have to build defences against too much exposure to massive human suffering; they have to get used to it. This necessary cynicism, as it were, has begun to operate as an alternative to Christian faith. Theology must address this deep layer of unfaith in believers and unbelievers alike. The intelligibility of the church's theology is at stake here because increasingly people can find no coherent intelligibility in history itself.

Secondly, the church's theology must address the question of human freedom on both its social and individual levels. This issue is intimately connected with the problem of the meaningfulness of history, but it also converges closely on the issue of Christian life and spirituality. There is a growing sense that human freedom is a power of creativity, the ability to plan and accomplish new things, distinctive and original things. The theology of creation, providence, grace and salvation as well as the role of the church and its ministry must be brought into correlation with this new human experience. The relevance of the church is at stake here. Increasing numbers of people find traditional church teaching on the Christian life irrelevant to actual life in the world today.

In sum, this thesis is against individualism in theology. Every theology that does not address the social and public character of human life in history is inadequate today.

Conclusion

The church is the natural place for Christian theology. Theology construes the world, human existence and God through the symbols of scripture and tradition which are preserved in the community called church. I can summarize how this task is to be carried out in a way distinctive to our time on the basis of four historical developments which have significantly influenced both the church and the discipline of theology, that is, the complexification and explosion of knowledge, historical consciousness and the ecumenical movement, the encounter with world religions and interreligious dialogue, and the population explosion and its attendant massive social suffering.

In responding to these historical developments we have discovered the following things: first, that theology in the church is not limited by the boundaries of the church. From the standpoint of the church, theology transcends the church. It deals with the whole sphere of reality itself from within the purview of the symbols of Christian revelation. Second, the church itself which is the natural home of theology cannot be restricted to any confessional communion today. The premises and values underlying the ecumenical movement, which reach back to the essence of apostolic faith, break open the necessary and legitimate role of authority within any particular Christian tradition. To be ecumenical, Christian theology must both attend to and transcend the specific authorities and magisteria of particular churches. The great church, in its long history and especially in its united future, is theology's primary context. Third, this Christian church co-exists with other religions in a new common human history. This new context imposes what might be called a dialogical situation. Christian theology in this situation will attend to the faiths of other peoples and, being influenced by them, reformulate its self-understanding accordingly. Fourth, and in common with other religions, human beings must address the elements of our common existence which are senseless, murderous and scandalous. God's revelation to human beings in this world is for human existence in this world. To be credible and relevant, theology must address the actual lives of human beings in this world by formulating its meaning in social-historical terms as well as interpersonal and transcendent terms.

Christian Tradition and Contemporary Society

Carl Reinhold Bråkenhielm

More than forty years ago Richard Niebuhr published his influential book *Christ and Culture*. His five types of relationships between the Christian community and its cultural environment became a highly influential typology – and so did the theme of Christianity and culture itself. It seems that it is no longer so. The theme – Christianity and culture, church and civilization, theology and secularization and the like – exploded as it were in many different subthemes, which today occupy at least an important part of the theological scene. The most prominent and prestigious couple is theology and natural science. Another – softer and tender – is theology and literature. Theology and psychology might also be mentioned. Somewhat in the background we may discern theology and sociology. In comparison to the flow of literature on the theme of theology and natural science, the flow of literature on the relationship between theology and the theories and results of sociology appears to be less strident. There are, of course, the works by Peter Berger and Robert Bellah. Helmut Peukart has presented an interesting theological interpretation of Jürgen Habermas. Still, I think that the queston of the relationship between Christian theology and basic sociological facts of contemporary society is not in the foreground as it used to be. It might be implicit in what many theologians do – but it is not, as it were, thematized in a way that evokes great interest.

In a way this is rather surprising, considering what Christian theologians often say Christian theology is about. Let me just take one example. In the methodological chapter of a highly influential theological textbook David Tracy summarizes the task of theology in the following way:

Theology is the attempt to establish mutually critical correlations between an interpretation of the Christian tradition and an interpretation of the contemporary situation.[1]

Now, if this indeed is the task of theology, then it is only reasonable that some substantial effort should be undertaken with regard to the question of Christianity and culture, especially the relationship between Christian tradition and the contemporary social situation.

Needless to say there is more than one interpretation of the Christian tradition. The one which forms the background of this article could be described as 'first-article Lutheran', affirming the creative activity of God preserving and renewing the world through basic human actions of concern and love. Jesus Christ is the prime example of those creative energies flowing forth and challenging the forces of destruction. However, the elaboration of this interpretation of Christianity is the subject-matter of a different article. My main concern in the present one is our understanding of the contemporary social situation.

The contemporary social situation can be undertood through the eyes of the social theorist. One example could be Jürgen Habermas and his theory of the colonization of the life-world by cohorts of experts. Given the adequacy of this theory, much could be said about the depreciation of ordinary everyday reality and the neglect of reproductive values that are essential to my 'first-article' Lutheran interpretation of Christianity. But I shall not pursue this line further. There is, however, another way to understand the contemporary social situation, i.e. through the eyes of ordinary men and women. We might ask the following question: what is the theological relevance of the world-views and values of ordinary men and women in today's world? Is the manner in which theology is done in any way affected by the things men and women value in their lives, their fundamental attitudes or the main convictions they have about human beings or even the universe as a whole? Many theologians would not simply dismiss these facts as theologically irrelevant. Maybe Karl Barth would – but it is at least interesting to note that David Tracy would seem not to. Tracy calls for an interpretation of 'those fundamental questions (finitude, estrangement, alienation . . . and so forth) that disclose a genuinely religious dimension in our contemporary experience and language'.[2] There are still many questions about this programme. Here are three of them:

1. How are we to gain knowledge about these 'fundamental questions'?
2. How do we 'detect a . . . religious dimension in our contemporary experience'?
3. And how do we decide if this dimension is 'genuine' or not?

I would like to offer some brief comments on each of these questions. I am very much aware of the immensity of at any rate the last two questions. But I am at least in a position to give a fairly precise suggestion as to how to answer the first one, i.e. the question about the fundamental questions in our contemporary experience and language. Broadly speaking, one could think of at least two different methods. The *first* one would be phenomeno-logical or existential, the second one empirical. The phenomenological method would rely upon a vision or intuition of the essential conditions of human beings – and the possible responses to these conditions. The paradigm of this method is found in Martin Heidegger and was later used by Rudolf Bultmann to sift out the timebound from the timeless in the Synoptic Gospels. The disadvantages of this method are well known. It relies upon an advanced metaphysics which – as is also well known – is not always as transparent as desired. The *second* method – the empirical – has the disadvantage of being less universal in its conclusions. But it does not require such a heavy load of metaphysics. This is the method we have applied at the Department of Faiths and Ideologies at the University of Uppsala in Sweden. Basically we have worked with the help of surveys and individual interviews. Here is not the place to go into the methodological details of these projects. Rather, I would like to give some idea of our basic concepts and most interesting results. I think that with some of these results in mind, I might be better equipped to make some suggestions about the religious dimension in these modern values and world-views – and at least offer a tentative insight into what might be genuinely religious in these values.

I

Most of these studies have been carried out by a group of scholars within the Department of Theology at the University of Uppsala. The real pioneer has been Professor Anders Jeffner. Others participating are Professor Thorleif Pettersson, Dr Eva Hamberg and myself. We have worked with surveys of representative samples of the Swedish population and with longer interviews of individual persons. Our starting-point has been a widely used definition of a life-philosophy proposed by Anders Jeffner. A life-philosophy is defined as a complex of a person's central values, basic attitudes and such cognitive elements which suggest a more comprehensive view of life. These three elements stand in a complicated relationship to one another. At the level of definition it seems reasonable to leave the question of the more exact character of this relationship open. But it is clear that values and norms often presuppose the truth of certain factual beliefs which may be a part of a world view.[3] It is therefore not surprising that a change in world-view is followed by a change of values. This is a well-known aspect of religious conversion, which could be defined as a sudden change of view of life.

The advantage of this definition is that it delimits an interesting field of study, which encompasses not only established belief-systems such as Christian doctrine or Marxist ideology, but also thoughts by ordinary men and women. This has been the focus of some of our recent projects. One was conducted already in 1987 with 400 personal interviews, with a view of obtaining a representative sample of the Swedish population. The aim of this project was to detect the central values, basic attitudes and comprehensive views of life in Sweden. Generally the interview lasted for an hour and was divided into two parts. Let me describe briefly some of the questions and some of the results.

1. *Central values.* One of the first questions in the interview was concerned with the central values of the respondents: 'When you reflect upon what is most important and significant in life, what do you think is most important?' The tendency in the answers to this question is clear: 90% mention something on the private level of life (only 5% have a central value of global character). And the majority takes health to be the most important thing in life. To be healthy is a central value. There are certain differences between different groups (age, sex, degree of materialism, etc.), but the main tendency is clear.

Another highly interesting idea of study concerns the value and dignity of human beings. From the great political ideologies of the nineteenth century we have inherited a salient anthropocentric perspective. This is inherent to the idea of human rights and the idea of the special value and dignity of human beings. It has been strong in the Swedish labour movement and has been one of the ideological forces behind the Swedish welfare system. One way to approach this issue is to ascertain people's ideas about the relationship between human beings and animals. Therefore, we formulated the following question to our respondents: 'Ought one to show greater respect for human beings than for other living creatures?' The answers to this question were unexpected. A majority (44%) answered in the *negative*; only 37% thought that human beings deserve greater respect than animals. To get a clearer idea of the motives behind these values, a smaller interview project was undertaken during the autumn of 1988. The results from this survey confirmed the former figures: two out of three persons in a representative sample (n = 521) of the Swedish population thought that human beings and animals are equally valuable. As a reason for this, most persons referred to the fact that we all belong to the same ecological system. But many were prepared to give animals such characteristics which traditionally had been exclusively reserved for human beings – such as having a soul, having self-consciousness and free will. (Recent studies in the 1990s show similar results.)

2. *Basic attitudes*. Let me now leave the question of central values and proceed to the issue of *basic attitude*. We tried to measure this elusive aspect of a life-philosophy in different ways. In the oral interview the respondents were asked to measure their satisfaction with life on a scale from 1 (low satisfaction) to 9 (complete satisfaction).

The main tendency is clear. We find an amazing contentment and satisfaction with life. People in Sweden today are simply happy. 77% claim that they are favoured, and only 6% deny the claim that they look towards the future with trust. One further thing can be noted. This positive basic attitude does not seem to be correlated with any particular value-system or world-view. This could be said to concide with the results of Milton Rokeach and his group of researchers.[4] They found that another aspect of the basic attitude, namely open and closed minds, does not vary with the *content* of different belief systems – open and closed minds rather affect the *way* in which, say, political ideology is affirmed.

3. *Comprehensive view of the world*. So much about the basic attitudes of common life-philosophies in Sweden today. The third element of a life-philosophy involved comprehensive ideas about the world, human beings and nature. Many questions in our interviews were designed to capture this aspect. One of the questions was formulated in the following way:

> Certain people have always reflected on the true nature of our reality. Some have come to the conclusion that nothing exists but matter in different forms. Others say that there is also a divine or spiritual reality of some sort. Do you reflect on these things?

An overwhelming majority (71%) gives a positive answer to this question. These persons are confronted with yet another question: 'Can you say anything about your conclusions?' Among the answers to this question, one can discern three distinctive groups. There is one group of materialists (n = 48), and another group of more or less traditional believers in God or a divine power (n = 54). But the great majority is – not surprisingly – in between. They are open to the transcendent, but have vague conceptions. A typical answer comes from a middle-aged woman in an earlier project. She replies to the question whether the interview has captured what she thinks is important in life:

Partly I have expressed most things, but it is difficult to describe inner feelings. Emotions and thoughts, sometimes contradictory, sometimes strong. Do I believe in God? – I don't know, but still I know that there is something, for example, in the unknown. Do I have moral values? – Yes, but why? What are they founded on? Is it only something I have been taught? It is difficult to find an answer.

In our research we have found that the neglected area between unbelief and belief is of considerable interest. An international study (European Value Study) has revealed that whilst Swedes in general are very reluctant to affirm a personal God (15%, 1990), 44% claim that they believe in a life-force or spirit of some kind. The opposite to Sweden in Europe is Ireland, where almost 65% believe in a personal God and only 25% in a life-force or spirit. In contrast to Ireland, the majority of the Swedes are outside traditional Christianity – but they are not outside religion.

Other issues concerning life after death and human nature were also covered in our project. Here I cannot deal with these problems. However, I wish to note just one particular aspect. In the interview the respondents were confronted with the following statement:

Human beings only consist of body and matter.

The respondents were given the opportunity to choose between three possibilities: complete agreement, partial agreement, and disagreement. 53% of the respondents disagreed. This is interesting, but more interesting are the differences between men and women in this respect.

Attitudes towards the statement that human beings only consist of body and matter. Percentage (n = 377)

Human beings consist only of body and matter	All	Men	Women
Complete agreement	20	30	9
Partial agreement	26	30	21
Disagreement	54	40	70

The differences between men and women in relation to this central issue of human nature call for further studies. Here is an interesting area for empirical feminist theology.

The overall picture could be described in the following way. One could speak of the emergence of an ecological life-philosophy. Central to many persons is the idea of the unity of life. Human beings are but a thread in the web of nature. Humans and animals are equal – at least in principle. Health – the health of the body – is the most important thing in life. Why? Because this is the only life I have and I want to make the most of it. This world-view is permeated by a basic attitude of optimism. Most people are satisfied with their lives – even if the recession has taken its toll. Somewhere there is an unclear sense of something more, that reality is greater and richer than the part of it that we can discern with our senses and capture through our concepts.

It would seem that this life-philosophy is rather remote from the central affirmations of traditional Christian belief. Traditional belief is anthropocentric – or theocentric – and not *biocentric*, as the general drift appears to be in Sweden. The optimistic basic attitude seems far removed from the consciousness of guilt and finitude affirmed by Lutheran orthodoxy. In the world-view there is a certain openness towards the transcendent; but it is mostly vague and uncommitted. For a foreigner it must come as a surprise that more than 95% of the Swedish population are members of the Lutheran state church! Customs seem more stubborn than beliefs.

II

Let me now proceed to the more difficult question of the theological interpretation of these results. How do we go about establishing 'mutually critical correlations between Christian tradition and the contemporary situation' which according to David Tracy is the central task of constructive theology? The difficulty with this question is that we might know a lot about the central Christian symbols and concepts and much about contemporary values and world-views, but still be unable to correlate these two fields in an interesting way. I am not confident that it is possible to make any illuminating correlation between Christian tradition and the life-philosophy of the Swedish people. Still, I want to offer some theological comments, and then ask if there is anything to learn from the way these comments were made. This may sound obscure, but I hope it will get clearer in a moment.

Let me begin with the central value of health. Health is the most important thing in life. Health is then to be understood not merely in terms of absence of disease – even if this is important – but also in terms of presence of contentment and a certain trust in the future. Perhaps it is the more sophisticated idea that if you stay healthy, i.e. without any major disease, and physically fit without overweight, you will be happy. This is still not clear. Now, let's hear the comment of the constructive theologian.

Starting with health we might link up with the central Christian symbol of salvation. And we may remind ourselves that in the ministry of Jesus, there is this strange relationship between health, salvation and forgiveness of sins. Is some theological contribution coming from this area? Well, some contemporary religious movements seem to be suggesting nothing less than this, i.e. linking health, salvation and financial success.

There is also another possibility. The ideal of health might be taken as something of an idol, an effort to strive for something that in the end will fail. The constructive theologian might tell us to secure our lives in something more permanent than the health of our frail organisms. Kjell Kellenberg – a colleague from Sweden – made the following comment:

> It seems that a life-philosophy which covers life in its painful manifoldness and which is coloured by a fundamental trust has a greater ability to give support in the difficult situations of life. There is an obvious risk that health as the meaning of life only gives meaning as long as you have health.

Another result in our survey was the amazing satisfaction and contentment with life in Sweden. As far as we can judge, the anxiety, guilt and estrangement of Ingmar Berman's *The Seventh Seal* is far away. The tendency is the same in many other Western countries (even if the Germans and the Italians are not as happy as the Swedes and the Dutch). This is interesting, because it goes against the ideas of many existentialists, who have underlined feelings of finitude and anxiety as basic existentials. Following Karl Jaspers, several theologians have taken up the idea of limiting experiences of guilt, death and suffering. The problem with this approach was clearly perceived by Dietrich Bonhoeffer. In his *Letters and Papers from Prison* he writes:

> I should like to speak of God not at the boundaries but at the centre, not in weaknesses, but in strength; and therefore not in death and guilt but in man's life and in goodness. As to the boundaries, it seems to me better to be silent and leave the insoluble unsolved.[5]

Bonhoeffer's point could be taken as a plea for a *theologia gloriae* and a devaluation of the *theologia crucis*. He could find a point of connection for his plea in the general sentiments in post-industrial Sweden. Still, this line of thinking is not without problems. It could be argued that the contentment and satisfaction of rich Westerners is deceptive and an aspect of what Karl Marx called 'false consciousness'. It takes on an ideological character when used by commercial interests and the media. The experience of happiness and goodness has to be distinguished from the wish-fulfilments of the consumer-society. In sum, there is no easy theological interpretation of the contentment reflected in our studies.

A third theological comment might be directed against the seemingly growing conviction that human beings and animals are equally valuable. First, it could be argued that this is clearly against the central Christian conviction that human beings alone are created in the image of God. The levelling of humans and animals can then be taken as the last step in the process of secularization. First, God was dethroned, put off the top of the pyramid as it were. Human being was left at the centre of the universe. Now, we perceive the dethronement of the human species. The last vestiges of the Christian tradition are disappearing. The human being becomes just a part of nature.

This might not be a very sensitive interpretation. There is certain evidence that leads us to believe that it is not so much humans that are being lowered to the level of animals, but rather animals that are being exalted to the level of humans. They are given all the attributes formerly reserved for human beings, i.e. free will, culture, self-consciousness, etc. This in turn might reflect a wider metaphysical world-view with roots which go a long way back in our history, i.e. the idea that everything is interrelated, that the world is an intricate web of life and that all things ultimately depend on a delicate balance which stands in danger of being disrupted by human beings. In another study based on longer interviews with ordinary men and women, I have several times heard references to the importance of the balance of nature. It is almost as if ecology and biology are being exalted to some kind of metaphysics.

Is there a religious dimension in this? Sometimes there seems to be an almost transcendent aspect to this ecological world-view. God is not exactly perceived as the Creator of the world, but rather as the Soul of the Universe. In this way one might discern a religious dimension in the affirmation of the equality between human beings and animals.

Let me now, briefly, reflect on the nature of these comments. I think I have used the symbol of the cross of Jesus or the symbol of creation and examined their capacity to illuminate, i.e. to enrich our understanding of what people mean when they affirm their ideal of health. I have tried to interpret contemporary values and world-views from the perspective of certain biblical stories, directed as we are by what these stories are about. The constructive theologian – to put it in a condensed way – uses central symbols and concepts from the Christian tradition in order to disclose a religious meaning and significance in contemporary values and world-views. Now, the difficulty with constructive theology is that it somehow requires three kinds of abilities. It requires the ability first critically to assess the symbols of Christian tradition, and secondly to have accurate knowledge of contemporary values and world-views. Thirdly – and most difficult – it requires some ability to correlate these two sources of knowledge critically, to disclose something of religious significance which goes beyond descriptive theology as well as the social sciences. The problem is that we might go wrong on any or all of these tasks.

III

A few words about the last question. If something of religious significance has been disclosed, *how do we judge whether we have disclosed 'a genuinely religious dimension in our contemporary experience and language'* (as Tracy puts it). This is really a philosophical and neither a theological nor a sociological question. It brings into focus the perennial issue of religious experience, the question of its nature and truth. Religious men and women claim that they experience God or Christ. But can we trust their claims? I have written extensively about this question elsewhere.[6] In the present context my comments must be shorter and more roughly hewn.

I suggested above that at one point we might detect the presence of a religious dimension in contemporary experience, namely in the ecological world-view, i.e. in the experience of oneness with nature and everything there is. Everything is interrelated and we are all parts of one whole, which ultimately goes beyond that which is measurable. Is this a genuine religious experience? I think many theologians and Christian believers would have some difficulty with this. They would sense what is condescendingly called 'pantheism'. The orthodox Christian would like to draw a clear ontological line between the creator and the creation and affirm the unilateral dependence of the latter upon the former. If we go along with this strict definition of Christianity, I guess that we are obliged to reject the kind of spirituality for which a good many Swedes and almost a third of the European population express a certain sympathy. I think it is a matter of considerable theological interest that many Swedes are drawn to more impersonal and pantheistic concepts of God.

Let me finally stress that there is a growing number of people – particularly among the younger generation – who do not consider themselves to be Christians at all. Such persons are not likely to be convinced that *any genuine* religious experiences can be disclosed *anywhere* by *any* kind of symbols or concepts. Of course, this is so only if we take the meaning of 'genuine' in a fairly strong sense, meaning the same as 'veridical' or 'non-illusory'. But 'genuine' can also be taken in a weaker sense, meaning the same as that which Peter Berger once called prototypical human gestures. Informed by his sociological research, Berger argued that there are a kind of anthropological universals, common human practices which are not so much part of what it means to be a Westerner or an African or an Indonesian, but rather part of what it is to be a human being. Berger wrote:

> By prototypical human gestures I mean certain reiterated acts and experiences that appear to express essential aspects of man's being, of the human animals as such.[7]

Berger argued that these prototypical gestures (or at least some of them) could be interpreted as signals of transcendence, phenomena that appear to point beyond the natural world to a deeper dimension of reality. He found such signals of transcendence in men's and women's ordering of the universe, their play, hope and humour, but also in their ultimate condemnation of evil.

Berger's book might be a good example of discerning the religious dimension in the data of modern sociological analysis. In contrast to the theologian he did not rely upon the disclosing power of central symbols in the Christian tradition. In this way he is a kind of analogy to the natural theologian, well known in the eighteenth century and to be found in places even today. But there is an interesting difference. It is no longer natural science that provides the point of departure – it is rather the social sciences. It might be that the theological relevance of the social sciences does not extend as far as the theological relevance of the natural sciences once did and still do for some theologians. Nevertheless, if social theory or sociological analysis can show that the grip of religion goes deeper than merely external allegiance to traditional religious authorities, then it appears that the religious believer is less vulnerable to the charge of irrationality. This would imply that sociological research into contemporary religion has more theological relevance than merely as a provider of background knowledge to Christian ministry and religious affirmations in general. It may even have some bearing on religious truth. The mere possibility of this suggests that sociological research deserves a stronger theological standing than it has today.

Notes

1. *Christian Theology: An Introduction to Its Traditions and Tasks*, ed. Peter C. Hodgson and Robert H. King, Philadelphia ²1989, 36.

2. Ibid., 53.

3. For further references see Arthur Danto, *Mysticism and Morality*, Harmondsworth 1976, Chapter 1.

4. See Milton Rokeach, *The Open and Closed Mind: Investigations into the Nature of Belief Systems and Personality Systems*, New York 1960.

5. Dietrich Bonhoeffer, *Letters and Papers from Prison. The Expanded Edition*, London and New York 1971, 282.

6. See Carl Reinhold Bråkenhielm, *The Problems of Religious Experience*, Stockholm 1985.

7. Peter L. Berger, *A Rumour of Angels: Modern Society and the Rediscovery of the Supernatural*, Harmondsworth 1970, 53.

II · The Programme of Theology

The Return of God in Contemporary Theology

David Tracy

I Introduction: *theos* and *logos* in *theo-logia*

The history of theology is the history of the ever-shifting relationship between the reality of God and that divine reality as experienced and understood from within a *logos*, i.e. a particular horizon of intelligibility. The theologian is one who attempts the nearly impossible task of correlating *theos* and *logos*. When that central responsibility is poorly executed, the *logos* of some contemporary intelligibility overwhelms and domesticates the reality of *theos*. Then theology – as in the modern period – becomes obsessed with finding exactly the right method, the irrefutable modern rational argument, the proper horizon of intelligibility for comprehending and perhaps controlling God. To be sure, insights continue to occur. Genuine arguments are forged. Brilliant speculations ensue. Better methods, more exact and exacting hermeneutics are developed. All the modern achievements of theology are indeed significant. But we are all, willingly or unwillingly, being forced to leave modernity. We leave it with genuine new insights, thanks to the modern *logos*, into the reality of God. Modern theology has forged an understanding of God understood as the uniquely relational individual. For God – and God alone – is related to all reality as the origin, sustainer and end of all reality. And yet many contemporary theologians who hold, as I do, that modern theology has indeed made a permanent contribution to the history of theology by forging various and increasingly sophisticated relational concepts to understand God's radically relational nature better than pre-modern theologies did not hesitate to affirm that achievement without further questioning. The awesome, frightening, interruptive reality of God can seem lost even in the best modern concepts forged to articulate the relational insights of modern theologies.

Contemporary theology can be called by many names. None of those names suffices, as the strange name 'postmodernity' makes clear. But, at its best, postmodern theology is an honest if sometimes desperate attempt to let God as God be heard again; disrupting modern historical consciousness, unmasking the pretensions of modern rationality, demanding that attention be paid to all those others forgotten and marginalized by the modern project. *Theos* has returned to unsettle the dominance of the modern *logos*. There can be little doubt that in modern theology the *logos* of modern intelligibility was the dominant partner in the correlation. There can also be little doubt that across many forms of contemporary theology the power of God is once again the dominant partner in the theological correlation. A brief historical reflection on this development may aid our present assessments.

II A theonomous question: who is God?

The question of God in the Scriptures is not primarily the question of the existence, nature and attributes of God but the question 'Who is God?' For the Christian that question is answered decisively in and through the event and person of Jesus Christ. In Jesus Christ, the sacrament of God, Christians discover both who God is and who they are commanded and empowered to become. Christians learn the identity of God by learning the identity of Jesus as the Christ. This identity Christians learn principally through the history-like realistic passion-narratives of the four Gospels.[1]

Each of the four Gospel narratives tells that story in a distinct, indeed different way: from the strange apocalyptic tale of Mark, through the wisdom narrative of Matthew and the realistic hero's quest of Luke to the meditative narrative of John and the disturbing, dialectical reflections on Christ crucified of Paul. Yet each biblical telling also renders a single identity: the identity of God is disclosed in and through this unsubstitutable Jesus; the identity of Jesus is disclosed through his narrated words and actions, his doings and sufferings, his cross and resurrection. The first great Christian metaphor for God – God is Love (I John 4.16) – occurs in the first letter-commentary on John's meditative Gospel. As the Gospel of John made clear through linking its theological meditations to the narrative of Jesus, the reality of God as Love can never be divorced, for the Christian, from the disclosure of God's reality and power in the narrated history of Israel, nor from God's wrath and suffering in Christ, nor from Jesus' lamentations toward God (My God, my God, why have you forsaken me?), nor from Jesus' vindication as the Christ in the resurrection.

There is little wonder that the early Christian theologians could find trinitarian language so fitting for their understanding of God – an understanding achieved in their liturgies and their lives by their experiences of God in the Spirit through the Word to the Father. It is also little wonder that Christian theologians, alive to the Greek horizon of intelligibility within which they lived and thought, could also find not only love but also intelligence so ready a clue to the nature of God whose identity they saw decisively disclosed in the Word, Jesus Christ. Through the whole patristic and mediaeval periods, these two central realities – intelligence and love – became the principal clues for understanding the nature of the God identified as Love in Jesus Christ. Scholastic theology would nicely name a partial, incomplete, analogous but real understanding of the Ultimate Mystery who is God through reflections on both intelligence and love. Some theologians – Augustine and Aquinas prominent among them – would develop these brilliant analogies of intelligence and love to help Christians understand a little more of the nature of God. Rarely since those theonomous times have theologians managed to allow the reality of the God disclosed in Jesus Christ to function so well. That divine reality was always illuminated but never controlled by the *logos* of Greek and Roman and mediaeval cultures on the nature of intelligence and love. Love as Greek *eros* was experienced and understood to be transformed by divine *agape* into Augustine's *caritas*. Human active intelligence was employed to provide some glimpse – however transitory – into a world of mathematical and dialectical intelligibility serving as an entry-point into the world of pure divine intelligence.[2] It is refreshing even today to read the still startling achievements of the great patristic and mediaeval theologians in under-standing the God of Jesus Christ by means of their transformation of the Greco-Latin *logos* on both love and intelligence. In some ways these earlier theonomous reflections on understanding God through understanding and transforming Greek love and intelligence are not merely permanent but unsurpassed and perhaps unsurpassable achievements. That remains the case at least until such time as theologians can glimpse again that earlier amazing and optmistic vision: the participatory understanding of all reality as sheer intelligibility and the whole cosmos as erotic. Only some forms of modern science – as Teilhard de Chardin saw – share that earlier optimism on reason and desire alike.

Even through the centuries dominated by these theonomous achieve-ments of understanding God as Love and Intelligence, however, two alternative unsettling undercurrents were always at work. The first undercurrent challenged even the highest achievements of the theologians employing Greek understandings of intelligence for attempting a better understanding of Godself as pure intelligence. Again and again the refrain occurs — above all in the great line from Dionysius the Areopagite through John Scotus Erigena through one side of Thomas Aquinas through Eckhart and Nicholas of Cusa. The incomprehensibility of God disclosed in and through God's very comprehensibility became an ever more radical testimony of increasing apophaticism. It functioned as a strong undercurrent become, finally, a powerful undertow to all theological confidence in the many uses of the *logos* of Greek intelligibility.

At the same time – now through apocalyptic movements and Pauline theologians of the cross – another and even more unsettling underground current drove much Western Christian theological reflection: the reality of God was revealed not in glory or *eros* or intelligence but in the hiddenness of the cross – i.e. God is revealed in the weakness, conflict, suffering of this Jesus Christ. All those Christians who could never forget the hidden God disclosed in Mark's troubled narrative and reflected upon in Paul's unrelenting dialectic of the cross awaited the day when this great undercurrent would resurface. Then it would function not as a powerful and unsettling undertow to all intellectualist theologies of God (like the apophatic traditions on divine incomprehensibility did) but more like a flood that invaded and finally overtook the consciousness of many Christians. As surely this Pauline-Markan insight did resurface in the profound sense of the hidden-revealed God of Luther, Calvin and Pascal. Here surely the new existential sense of *theos* as revealed in the hiddenness of the cross almost overwhelmed the *logos* of prior ages on love and intelligence. Indeed at times this existential experience of God's revelation only in hiddenness came close to overwhelming any cultural horizon of understanding at all. Hence all formal appeals to reason, to intelligence, to eros were abandoned in favour of the hidden God in Luther's brilliant and intense theological outbursts of Pascal's terror at the silence of infinite space at the very dawn of modernity. On the whole, however, as modernity took over, all these currents went underground again as the modern *logos* took over *theo-logia* and recast the understanding of God into properly modern terms.

III God within the modern *logos*: from deism to panentheism

The hidden God of Luther, so explosive in the Reformation, was transformed in early modernity into a profoundly anxious sense of the silence of infinite space in Pascal. Indeed Pascal is the quintessential early modern who, almost alone, saw both modernity's overpowering strength and its destructive power at eliminating the very sense of God's reality. The Godhead beyond God of Eckhart also went underground again after a last brilliant efflorescence in the most balanced of the great Renaissance thinkers, Nicholas of Cusa – the only theologian in whom the *logos* of mathematical intelligibility, the sense of infinity in early Renaissance modernity and the apophatic tradition united into one last great outburst of a neo-Platonic, an oddly optimistic *'docta ignorantia'*.[3] In the meantime, the relentless progress of modernity took over all thought, including the thought of God.

The difficulty of modernity on the question of God can now be seen with clarity. So strong, so new, so powerful was the modern *logos* – that horizon of intelligibility encapsulated in the modern scientific revolution and the modern turn to the subject of Descartes and Kant and climaxing in the classic modern democratic revolutions and the emergence of modern historical consciousness – that no question could be allowed to be free of radical rethinking by so amazing a constellation of cultural strength and political-economic achievement united to equally amazing intellectual narrowness.

The reality of God was recast as a modern question in order to be properly understood by a modern mind. Those who still possessed a strong sense of God's reality as central to their lives became, as Michel de Cerreau has shown, marginal to the modern centralizing project. Indeed such intensely religious persons became what moderns now called 'mystics'. An adjectival dimension to life and culture (the 'mystical') now became a modern noun, the 'mystic'. This noun was used to name the large group of outsiders to the modern project. All reality must be disciplined by modern thought, including the reality of God and religion.

The modern God became the captive of one or another modern 'ism'. For the *logos* of modernity – its powerful notion of intelligiblity – found a new way to understand God, more exactly a new series of ways. On the question of God, the modern mind had choices, to be sure. But all the modern choices were principally determined not by the reality of God but by the *logos* of modernity. A modern could, for example, be a deist or a modern theist or artheist or agnostic. A modern could become, with Spinoza, a modern pantheist or, with Hegel and Whitehead, a modern panentheist.

There can be no doubt that these modern understandings of God yielded genuine insights into the reality of God. This is especially the case on the question of panentheism. For it was in modern theology – including modern Trinitarian theologies – that the intrinsically relational character of all reality, including, indeed especially, the divine reality, could be understood with the kind of conceptual clarity lacking in ancient and mediaeval 'God-talk'. Modern relational God-talk – Hegelian, process, trinitarian, modern feminist – solidified as the one permanent achievement of modern theologies of God.

And yet even this now classic modern achievement came with a high price: in both Hegel and Whitehead, in many forms of modern relational thought (including several forms of feminist relational thought on God), the question recurs: is God rendered a conceptual prisoner of a new intellectual system of totality with no real moment of infinity allowing God to be God? Even that quintessential modern thinker, René Descartes, managed, almost despite himself, to allow God's infinity to break through his modern totality system. Does infinity break through Hegel or Whitehead or other contemporary modern forms of radically relational systematic (totalistic?) understandings of God?

Even modern theology's greatest achievement in understanding God – the relationality of God and all reality – was always in danger of becoming one more system, one of a long line of modern 'isms'. Those 'isms' begin in early modernity, with an anti-relational 'deism', and end in late modernity with various relational forms of 'panentheism'. This is also the end of the contemporary story in the understanding of God unless one allows God's reality to break through the modern *logos* again. That breakthrough, indeed that radical interruption, is the central meaning of postmodern contemporary thought on God.

IV Postmodernity and the strange return of God

By its attack upon the self-confidence of the modern *logos*, postmodernity provided a new opportunity for serious contemporary thought on God. To be sure, much contemporary thought will continue to be modern in character and achievement: as in the sensitive and impressive reflections on God in cosmology and some of the 'new physics' or in the renewed question of God for many modern scientists and theologians in their mutually informative conversations on science. Much contemporary thought on God, moreover, will prove to be a rediscovery of pre-modern forms for understanding God – as in the recent rediscovery of biblical narrative for Christian God-talk. At the same time, the most characteristic-ally postmodern forms of God-talk have allowed the awesome reality of *theos* to return in force after postmodernity's calling into question of modernity's powerful *logos*.

Indeed, postmodernity tends to be suspicious of almost all traditional and modern arguments on the existence and nature of God, all attempts to fit God's reality into a modern horizon of intelligibility, all of the famous modern 'isms' for God, from deism and theism through panentheism. Postmodern thought believes that too much of modernity's self-confidence as a *logos* is ill-conceived. Indeed the central meanings of two of the central categories in the modern *logos* – history and language – have been shattered by the analyses of postmodern thought.

First, history. Historical consciousness is one of the great discoveries and achievements of modern thought. Too often, however, that historical consciousness has included a not so secret narrative history of its own: a social evolutionary schema whereby all history leads to 'the Western moderns'. All else is prehistorical, or 'primitive', or 'archaic', or on its way to becoming another, if lesser, version of Western modernity.

History, on the modern schema, is a linear, continuous, teleological schema with a single *telos* – Western modernity. In such a schema, God (disguised as one or another modern 'ism') is part of the schema: a sometimes important part (theism and panentheism) or sometimes missing part (atheism and agnosticism), but a part nonetheless. But what if history is not continuity at all, but constituted by detours and labyrinths and radical interruptions? What if the modern social evolutionary teleological schema underlying modern self-understanding is exposed as both imperialist and implausible? Indeed modernity's sense of continuity and confidence has been shattered by two unassimilable elements – the interruption of massive global suffering in modern history and the interruption of all those others set aside, forgotten and colonized by the grand narrative of Eurocentric modernity. The meaning of suffering, the reality of the others and the different: those are the realities that destroy the teleological version of modern history and allow for the return of the eschatological God disrupting all continuity and confidence.

God enters postmodern history not as a consoling 'ism' but as an awesome, often terrifying, hope beyond hope. God enters history again not as a new speculation – even a modern trinitarian one! – but as God. 'Let God be God' becomes an authentic cry again. For this God reveals Godself in hiddenness: in cross and negativity, above all in the suffering of all those others whom the grand narrative of modernity has set aside as non-peoples, non-events, non-memories, non-history.

God comes first as empowering hope to such peoples and theologies: a God promising to help liberate and transform all reality and promising as well to challenge and overcome the self-satisfied *logos* of modernity. God also comes to these postmodern forms of contemporary theology not only as the hidden-revealed God of the hope in the cross, in the memory of suffering and the struggle by, for, and with 'others' – especially the forgotten and marginal ones of history. God also comes as an ever deeper hiddenness – the awesome power, the terror, the hope beyond hopelessness often experienced in the struggle for liberation itself. Thus does the God of Job speak out of the whirlwind again in Gustavo Gutiérrez's profound later reflections on the hidden-revealed God. Thus does 'suffering unto God' and lamentation towards God emerge as a resistance to all modern speculation on God in the post-Auschwitz, later political *theo-logia* of Johann Baptist Metz.[4] The hidden-revealed God at its most fearsome and radical has re-entered theological thought again. But that entry is now not through the estranged and alienated self of the existentialist theologians, those admirable and deeply troubled moderns. The entry of the hidden-revealed God now comes through the interruptive experience and memory of suffering itself, the suffering of all those ignored, marginalized and colonized by the grand narrative of modernity. In the light of that interruption, the modern 'isms' for God suddenly seem somewhat inconsequential. In that interruption the apocalyptic God of power, hope and awe often becomes the God of lamentation and Job returns to undo the power of the modern *logos* over 'God' in contemporary theologies.

At the same time, the second category, language, has come in ever new and self-interrupting guises to disrupt modern thought in its own way. The very language which modern thought needs to think its horizon of intelligibility – its logocentric *logos* rendering God into one more modern 'ism' – disrupts modernity's sense of continuity and control. Through postmodern linguistic reflections on the unthought factors in modern thought, the modern *logos* dissolves its own former certainties and disowns its own self-presence and self-grounding. The modern self is not whole enough to be as purely autonomous as it once thought itself. The modern *logos* is not stable enough to control the reality of the God it once seemed to manage so easily through its arguments from modern reason. God returns to remove the '*theos*', at once grounding and domesticated, in modernity's onto-*theo*-logy. God returns to demand that modernity disown once and for all its speculative ambitions to control the divine reality in order to let God be God again.

Moreover, the two classic clues for understanding God's reality – love and intelligence – also return in new, postmodern forms and sometimes formlessness. 'God is Love' now becomes an occasion not to show the reasonableness and relationality of the divine reality to the 'modern mind'. Love enters postmodernity first as transgression, then as excess, and finally as the transgressive excess of sheer gift.[5] To recover the great tradition of Dionysius the Areopagite again – the tradition of God beyond Being – is not merely to call to task that early and partial harbinger of modern rational theology, Thomas Aquinas, for his great reversal of the Dionysian order of 'good' over 'being' for naming God. To retrieve the Dionysian tradition is also to challenge modern theology in all its characteristic forms at the root. For the God who is love is beyond being and transcendentality, beyond rationality and relationality. God is love – excess, gift, the Good. That is a thought which modern theology cannot think without yielding its *logos* to *theos* in ways it does not seem to know how to do. *Job* and *Lamentations* return to haunt contemporary theologians as they attempt to name God in the new hidden-revealed theologies focussed on history as interruption. So too such texts as the Song of Songs and the splendid feminist retrievals of God as Sophia return to be heard in ways modern theologies did not envisage as even possible, much less desirable.[6] But desire, body, love, gift have all returned to try to allow God-as-God to be named anew.

When one turns to the second classical clue for understanding God, intelligence, the situation is the same; the modern *logos* in modern theology can no longer control God. Another kind of transgression and excess occurs: not new reflection on love as gift but the kind of radical detachment attendant to a profoundly apophatic theology like that of Meister Eckhart. These postmodern namings of a Godhead beyond God disclose modern theology's inability to envisage God beyond its own logos. Soon cries of atheism and Buddhism are heard.

But just as the tragic character of history emerges in the new apocalyptic theologies trying to recover Mark's Gospel as well as Lamentations and Job, so too an insistence on attentiveness (that lost virtue and spiritual exercise) returns to clarify our contemporary needs. Indeed, in the apophatic piety of postmodern namings of God one can hear again what Simone Weil insisted moderns most needed to learn again: 'attentiveness without an aim is the supreme form of prayer'. Postmodern theology, at its best, is not a rival set of propositions to modern theology. It is something else: a search for entirely alternative forms. Even when speculative, postmodern thought is less propositional than it is an attempt at new forms of language rendering excess, gift, desire, prayer. The prayer and the forms can vary greatly from the attentiveness and detachment of apophaticism to the lamentation, awe and sometimes terror of apocalypticism. This may not be so unhappy a message for modern theology to hear after all: to hear again Job and Lamentation, the Song of Songs and Sophia, to sense a Godhead beyond God and surely beyond the many 'isms' created by and for the modern *logos*.

No one knows, I believe, where those post-modern suspicions and retrievals will finally lead. But this much is clear: amidst all the shouting of the present, the reality of God has returned to the centre of theology. This is not the time to rush out new propositions on the reality of God. This is rather the time to allow wonder again at the overwhelming mystery of God – as some physicists and cosmologists seem so much more skilled at doing than many theologians are. This is the time for theologians to learn to disallow the *logos* of modernity to control their thoughts on God as we learn anew to be attentive to God. We must learn somehow, in God's absent presence, to be still and know that God is God.

Notes

1. Hans W. Frei, *The Identity of Jesus Christ*, Philadelphia 1975.
2. See the splendid work of Bernard Lonergan here: *Verbum: Word and Idea in Aquinas*, London 1968.
3. Louis Dupré, *Passage to Modernity: An Essay in the Hermeneutics of Nature and Culture*, New Haven 1994.
4. Johann Baptist Metz, 'Suffering unto God', forthcoming in *Critical Inquiry*, Summer 1995; see also Gustavo Gutiérrez, *On Job: God-Talk and the Suffering of the Innocent*, Maryknoll 1987.
5. See Jean-Luc Marion, *God Without Being*, Chicago 1993.
6. Elizabeth Johnson, *She Who Is: The Mystery of God in Feminist Theological Discourse*, New York 1992.

Beyond the End of History?

Nicholas Lash

I Considering what lies ahead

'Where there is no escape, people ultimately no longer want to think about it. This eschatological ecofatalism allows the pendulum of private and political moods to swing in *any* direction. The risk society shifts from hysteria to indifference and vice versa.'[1] Not all the voices that we hear, of course, are variants of fatalism, aspects of despair. There are still many people whose imaginations are tuned to some kind of optimism by the mythical conviction that modern industrial society, with 'its thinking in categories of economic growth, its understanding of science and technology and its forms of democracy', represents a 'pinnacle' of human achievement 'which it scarcely makes sense even to consider surpassing. This myth has many forms of expression. Among the most effective is the mad joke of the *end of history*.'[2]

Defending his original thesis, Francis Fukuyama insisted that 'What I had suggested had come to an end was not the occurrence of events, even large and grave events, but History: that is, history understood as a single, coherent, evolutionary process, when taking into account the experience of all peoples in all times.'[3] By this, Fukuyama might have meant that this long century's suffering had cured us of the illusion that 'History' had ever happened; that we (*whoever* 'we' may be) might ever reasonably deem all other societies, past and present, inferior to our own. Unfortunately, notwithstanding his wistful recognition that 'The end of history will be a very sad time', with little left for human beings (or, perhaps, white American males?) to do except be caretakers of 'the museum of history', Fukuyama still supposes there to be no thinkable alternative to an historicist understanding of history as a tale of 'progress', an 'evolution from primitive to modern'.[4]

Writing at the end of World War II, Karl Popper recognized that the impulses of historicism were, in part, theological in character. 'It is,' he said, 'often considered a part of the Christian dogma that God reveals Himself in history; that history has meaning; and that its meaning is the purpose of God . . . I contend that this view is pure idolatry and superstition.'[5] Fukuyama would, I suspect, find this provocative fulmination unintelligible: for him, as for many inmates of supposedly 'secular' societies, the business of religion is, like the provision of cold beer, a matter of satisfying particular consumer preferences. Hence his belief that, except in territories influenced by Islam, 'religious impulses' have been 'successfully satisfied within the sphere of personal [i.e. private] life that is permitted in liberal societies'.[6]

As the collapse of Communism coincides with rapidly diminishing confidence in the ideals and visions of Enlightenment, and the construction of a single global system of production, information and exchange goes hand in hand with recognition of the irreversibility of damage inflicted on the ecosystem of which we form a part, consideration of the way ahead has rarely seemed so urgent, so uncertain, or so difficult to undertake.

When economists and social theorists, political scientists and experts in international relations, gather to discuss these things, they usually do not invite theologians to take part in the conversation. It is not simple prejudice which leads to this omission so much as the characteristically modern belief that the subject-matter of theology is religion, and that the business of religion is with the private heart rather than the public world.

Theologians will, of course, if they are wise, nevertheless insist on joining in the conversation, on the grounds that the subject-matter of theology is, *not* 'religion', but rather 'all things' – from their first beginning to their final end – considered in relation to the mystery of God: *sub ratione Dei*.[7]

We shall, in due course, consider why it is as misleading to imagine that our 'end' lies simply in some distant future as it would be to suppose that our 'beginning' now lies far behind. The Omega of our existence is its Alpha, God's eternal Word once uttered, the Crucified and Risen One, 'who is and who was and who is to come'.[8] Nevertheless, the forms of Christian reflection on, and planning for, the future of the world are, naturally and properly, shaped by eschatology: by expectations of the end.

According to Carl Braaten, 'Christianity today stands at the crossroads between two diametrically opposed interpretations of eschatology': on the one hand, consideration of events irrupting from another world in some near or distant future and, on the other, the dramatization of social-ethical objectives sought within this world.[9] While acknowledging that such dichotomies are false, he seems uncertain as to how they might most truthfully be overcome. As in much contemporary theology, this uncertainty is rooted in a tendency to treat the issues in dangerous abstraction from the actual contexts in which they arise. Thus, for example, the principal reasons that Braaten advances for 'the emphasis on eschatology in today's theology' are 'the general philosophical discovery of the phenom- enon of hope in human existence' and 'the historical rediscovery of the eschatological core of the message of Jesus'.[10] Nothing here about the grounds of these discoveries in the collapse of nineteenth-century Europe's dreams of endlessly expanding power and wealth; no mention of Passchendaele and Auschwitz, or of the impact of the recognition that the web of life on this small planet is not only finite but already damaged beyond repair by our bizarre performance.

Joseph Ratzinger, on the other hand, while strenuously resisting 'the transformation of eschatology into political messianism',[11] by no means underestimates the social and, indeed, cosmic implications of Christian hope. And a dispassionate observer might suppose there would be scope for fruitful conversation between his principle that 'The Kingdom of God is not a *political* norm of the political, but it is *a moral* norm of the political' and this suggestion from Jürgen Moltmann: 'Political theology is the internal critique of the modern world. Liberation theology is the external critique of the modern world. Is it not time for the critical theology of the First World and the Liberation Theology of the Third World to enter into some sort of alliance?'[12] When all is said and done, moral critiques of politics are ineluctably political in connotation.

We do not live, nor can we see, beyond the end of history. It is in time alone, the time that God has given us, that we are born, and live, make plans, build cities, cherish or destroy the world, find hope or else despair, and die. In the remaining sections of this article, I shall briefly comment, under three heads, on the contribution that theology might make to the consideration of our common future. The hope that Christianity deems 'theological' (that is, expressive of the relations with the mystery of God that human beings may, by God's grace, enjoy) first, in lifting us from the despair, takes us also beyond optimism; secondly, it takes us beyond the fantasy of science fiction to a more sober vision of the future of the world; and, thirdly, in liberating us from determinism, it enables us to live beyond control.

II Beyond Optimism

It is very frightening to gaze upon the prospects for the world: to be attentive to the sounds of alienated, frightened, self-contempt emanating from our cities; to listen to the cries of those, especially the old and very young, the causes of whose destitution are not (as we sometimes say) 'natural' disaster, but political and economic choices enacted elsewhere, by other people, at another time; to take seriously the imperviousness to transformation of the structures of the global market; to bear in mind that 'ecological disaster and atomic fallout ignore the borders of nations. Even the rich and powerful are not safe from them.'[13] Clear-sightedness demands that we admit that, as things at present stand, there seems no chance of bringing off, within the necessary time-scale, those comprehensive transformations of heart, and will, and institution, that the healing of the world requires.

And yet, in my experience, discussions amongst 'experts' of what the future holds in store usually conclude with unwarranted expressions of optimism. The seldom quite explicit dialogue goes like this: 'We will make out', 'How so?' 'Because the alternative is quite unthinkable.' Optimism is, in other words, often little more than a stoically courageous whistling against despair.

Thus, for example, the international lawyer Philip Allott, in a most intelligent and original study, while admitting that 'it may be too late to stop, still less to undo, the havoc caused by international unculture',[14] nevertheless affirms that 'It is a purpose of the present study to suggest that society is, indeed, naturally capable of being progressive, able to achieve its survival and prospering by the appropriate willing and acting of human beings.'[15]

One reason why secular narratives of optimism are so unconvincing is that, *as* narratives, they lack coherence. Still trapped in the 'modern' predilection for explaining things from no particular standpoint, they oscillate between impersonal abstraction and arbitrary personal testimony. Hence the importance of the increasing recognition that all theories are abbreviated forms of *someone's* story; that each of us is accountable for the stories that we tell, and that all our stories are ungrounded in the sense that they make tacit metaphysical appeals.[16]

Many people imagine that Christian theologians suppose themselves to possess all sorts of *information* about the future which other people lack. The fact of the matter is, however, that sensible Christians know themselves nescient: set to life-long discipline of learning to see in the dark. To hope in God, in Christian terms, is to know that God's creation has, in God's love, its future; it is not to know the forms that future takes. Hence Karl Rahner's insistence that 'eschatological assertions' are not to be read as 'previews of future events', and that '*Docta ignorantia futuri* is from the outset the theme that is proper to the theologian'.[17]

Telling the story of the world within that world's continuing history demands a kind of reticence. Concerning the details of the outcome of the world, in God, we have no information now that Jesus lacked in Gethsemane.[18] What we do have, in the gift of the Spirit of the risen Christ, is the ability to 'keep awake and pray'. It is the characteristic weakness of both optimism and despair that, lacking the discipline of hope, they take it upon themselves to furnish the story with the ending which it has not yet achieved. Both optimism and despair claim to 'have the answer' to the question of the future, whereas Christian hope, knowing that the answer lies in God, rests in the nescience of prayer 'Thy kingdom come'.[19]

And, in the meantime within the bounds of time, our task – in ethics and in politics, domestically and ecologically – is healing (which is what *salus* or 'salvation' means). And, as every doctor knows, the work of healing is not made less urgent, less specific, less demanding, by the mere fact that the bodies and the minds we are required to heal are finite.

III Beyond science fiction

Salus means healing. But what is it that needs healing, that (according to God's promise) is to be made whole, complete, secure? Amongst the many answers given to such questions, I shall mention two: 'us' and 'everything'.

First, consider 'us'. Who are 'we'? I propose a rule for reading sentences that contain this little word. Whenever the word 'we' is being used, ask three questions: Whom do those using it have in mind? Whom do they suppose that they have in mind? Whom should they have in mind?

As Christians considering 'salvation' we *should* have in mind no group more restricted than the human race. Where the future is concerned, even considerations of self-interest now alert us to this need: 'The potential for self-endangering developed by civilization in the modernization process' makes 'the utopia of a world society a little more real or at least more urgent'.[20]

The range of reference of the 'we' we use, as Christians, must, however, be as comprehensive in memory as in hope. All evolutionary accounts of human history, accounts that look only forwards from where the speaker stands, all utopian fantasies, all sunlit futures forgetful of the past, are disallowed, subverted by the silent witness of shed blood. 'We' are all those corpses shaded by the arms outstretched on Calvary.[21]

Among the more important lessons being learnt at the present time is that even 'all of humankind' is too small an answer to the question: What does God's love heal, make safe, bring to fulfilment in his peace? 'Everything' would be a better answer. Out of nothing, God makes everything, and what God's love makes that same love heals. We may be better placed to understand this than our predecessors were, because the whole system of the world has irreversibly become one single fact, increasingly becomes one artefact, one context, work-place, market, home or burial ground. And we first *saw* this, thirty years ago, in the astonishing beauty of those first pictures of the planet photographed from space.

It is sometimes suggested that the 'universalism' which is so striking a feature of twentieth-century theology has arbitrarily ignored or set aside the traditional doctrine of hell. On the one hand, however, the rejection, in the tradition, of *apocatastasis* was not an affirmation that hell was well populated but a denial of the possibility of conversion after death.[22] On the other hand, to exclude the possibility that the screws of self-obsession can be turned so tightly as to render us impregnable to God's transforming generosity would be too easily to set aside the evidence of destructive arrogance and cruelty which makes the world, throughout its history, a kind of Golgotha, a place of skulls.

The stories told by scientists play a larger part in shaping the imagination of the modern world than tales told by theologians. There are, moreover, influential scientists who endorse the physicist Paul Davies' claim that 'science offers a surer path to God than religion'. But, from Stephen Hawking to John Barrow and Frank Tipler, the God thus sought seems little more than an idea or explanation: at most, a distant, still intelligence.[23]

There is, in the writings of some most distinguished scientists (especially in their final chapters!), much irresponsible speculation of the kind that, when indulged in by philosophers and theologians, gives 'metaphysics' a deservedly bad name.[24] Moreover, just as some scientists presume the physics of the world's beginning to supersede doctrines of creation, so others presume their speculation about the future to supersede Christian eschatology. Thus Barrow and Tipler classify their efforts as 'physical eschatology', defined as 'the study of the survival and behaviour of life in the far future'.[25]

Christian eschatology is, however, no more about the distant future than the doctrine of creation is about the distant past. Just as Christian confession of all things' createdness *ex nihilo* makes no empirical claims concerning the initial conditions of the system of the world, but simply acknowledges the absolute dependence of everything there is upon the mystery which we call God, so also Christian confession that, in the end, all things are with God, warrants no speculation as to the way that things will be, but simply celebrates the world's fulfilment in God's peace.

The purely speculative character of the scientists' myths is, however, their least harmful feature. By appeal to principles such as 'Anything that cannot be read and understood as a Christological assertion is not a genuine eschatological assertion',[26] Christian eschatology is anchored to particularity, its business being with the *sense* of finitude, the Emmanuel-value of the flesh. Undisciplined to such sobriety, some scientists give vent to dangerous fantasies of disembodied and infinite power. These come in different versions, but they have in common an overestimation of the purity and the power of 'pure' intelligence, a disdain for the flesh, a terror of mortality.

'Complete knowledge,' we are told, 'is just within our grasp. Comprehension is moving across the face of the earth, like a sunrise.' In case we had not noticed the Promethean overtones, a molecular biologist adds: 'What comprehension and powers over nature Omega Man will command can only be suggested by man's image of the supernatural.' (He apparently has not heard that man's best image of the supernatural is a dead Jew swinging on a Roman gibbet.) On the road to Omega, 'It is conceivable that in another 10^{10} years, life could evolve *away from flesh and blood*' until, with 'the advantage of containing no organic material at all', we shall find 'freedom from the biological ball and chain'.[27]

The notion that these writings convey, 'that our natural, earthly life can be despised is not just meaningless; it is disastrous . . . It promotes, here and now, a distorted idea of what a human being essentially is.'[28] And yet, in my experience, this material is too seldom subjected to the philosophical and theological criticism that it deserves.

IV Beyond control

The belief that 'History' has ended implies that, at least from now on, it would be a mistake to imagine that any paticular event could make a fundamental difference to the way things went. Here, Fukuyama's Hegelianism joins hands in disillusion with at least some versions of post-modern nihilism, dismally chorusing that 'there is nothing new under the sun'.[29]

It is uncumbent upon Christians, confronting such exhaustion, and the unconcern and cynicism which it breeds, 'to resist the drift into a state of mind which regards all that passes before it as a kind of play, run for its interpretation, empty in itself of deep and drastic significance, except that significance be one which, in the mood of our generation, we impose upon it'.[30] It is, however, no less imperative to avoid falling into the trap of supposing that, *because* something of absolute significance is acknowledged to occur, in this or that particular place, on this or that particular occasion, *therefore* the new age which this event initiates must be protected, and its memory kept pure, through structures and institutions of control.

Lenin knew where he was going, knew in which direction he had set his face. He and his followers ascribed absolute significance to their achievement that October, during those 'ten days that shook the world'. Subsequently, that ascription was transmuted into the tyranny of Bolshevism, the system of control protective of the fact and memory of that achievement.

Soviet Communism has now collapsed, its illusory absolutism crumbling into the relativities of history. Yet, from its rise and fall, there are disturbing lessons to be learnt. 'Lenin knew where he was going. Are we to say less of Jesus?' However illusory the absoluteness of the October Revolution may have been, 'it is very hard to see how anything which we can continue significantly to call Christianity can survive the withdrawal of the predicate *final* from the work of Christ'.[31]

The challenge to Christianity – to its social practice and to its images and narratives of hope – is to sustain that recognition of absolute finality without the aid of those institutions and intellectual habits of authoritarian control to which the eschatological character of its belief has too often rendered it susceptible. In our own day, Teilhard de Chardin, whose voice many found attractively prophetic of the 'Omega', serves as a chilling instance of such perversion. This was the man who welcomed the production of the atomic bomb as evidence of teamwork; the man who said, in 1936: 'Fascism may possibly represent a fairly successful small-scale model of tomorrow's world. It may perhaps be a necessary stage in the course of which men have to learn, as though on a small training-ground, their human role.'[32]

In the cultures of modernity, Christian consideration of the future of the world has too often either been reactive – a matter of dancing to tunes composed by other people – or else, through dualistic dissociation of spirituality from politics, has supposed that it has nothing in particular to say (nothing, that is, more interesting than abstract disapproval).

It is, however, possible that 'the pathos of modern theology is its false humility'; that, with the supposed neutrality of secular reason decoded as ideology (an ideology, moreover, knowing no options other than either chaos or control), a Christianity converted towards trust in God might find the tranquillity and confidence in which to offer to the world the promise, and the practice, and the poetry of given peace, 'the discourse of non-mastery'.[33]

Now, as in the time of the gospel's first appearing, it is always and only along the *via dolorosa* that this offer is enacted, this peace outpoured.

None of us, however, – no individual and no social form, especially the form we call 'the church' – knows the extent to which, along that road, we are companions of the crucified or collaborators in his crucifixion. The history of Christianity is a history of people passing to and fro beneath the image, on the doorway's tympanum, of final judgment: 'In the midst of history, the judgment of God has already happened. And either the Church enacts the vision of paradisal community which this judgment opens out', or else it becomes an 'anti-Church', confining Christianity, 'like everything else, within the cycle of the ceaseless exhaustion and return of violence'.[34] God's peacefulness, which is the end of history, is gift and promise, but it is also absolute command.

Notes

1. Ulrich Beck, *Risk Society. Towards a New Modernity*, London 1992, 37.

2. Ibid., 11.

3. Francis Fukuyama, *The End of History and the Last Man*, London 1992, xii.

4. Fukuyama, 'The End of History?', *The National Interest* 16, 1989, 18; 'A Reply to my Critics', *The National Interest* 18, 1989–1990, 23.

5. Karl Popper, *The Open Society and its Enemies. Vol. II. The High Tide of Prophecy: Hegel, Marx, and the Aftermath*, London [5]1966, 271.

6. Fukuyama, 'The End of History?', 14.

7. See Thomas Aquinas, *Summa Theologiae*, Ia, 1.7.

8. Revelation 1.8.

9. Carl E. Braaten, 'The Kingdom of God and the Life Everlasting', *Christian Theology. An Introduction to its Traditions and Tasks*, ed. Peter C. Hodgson and Robert H. King, Philadelphia 1982, 293.

10. Ibid., 275.

11. Aidan Nichols, *The Theology of Joseph Ratzinger*, Edinburgh 1988, 167.

12. Joseph Ratzinger, *Eschatologie. Tod und Ewiges Leben*, Regensburg 1977, 59; Jürgen Moltmann, 'Political Theology and Liberation Theology', *Union Seminary Quarterly Review* 45, 1991, 217.

13. Beck, *Risk Society*, 23.

14. Philip Allott, *Eunomia. New Order for a New World*, Oxford 1990, 385.

15. Ibid., 105. Much hangs, admittedly, on how 'naturally' is construed.

16. On the importance of accountability, see Alasdair MacIntyre, *Three Rival Versions of Moral Enquiry*, London 1990, 201; on 'the critical non-avoidability of the theological and metaphysical', see John Milbank, *Theology and Social Theory. Beyond Secular Reason*, Oxford 1990, 3.

17. Karl Rahner, 'The Hermeneutics of Eschatological Assertions', *Theological Investigations* IV, London 1966, 328; 'The Question of the Future', *Theological Investigations* XII, London 1974, 181.

18. See Nicholas Lash, *Believing Three Ways in One God. A Reading of the Apostles' Creed*, London 1992, 120.

19. Matthew 6.10; 26.41. For an attempt to explore the contrast between the *praxis*

of Christian hope as a form of the tragic vision and Marx's endemic optimism, see Nicholas Lash, *A Matter of Hope. A Theologian's Reflections on the Thought of Karl Marx*, London 1981, esp. 248–72.

20. Beck, *Risk Society*, 47.

21. See, for example, Johann Baptist Metz's discussion of 'the future in the memory of suffering', in *Faith in History and Society*, London 1980, 100–18.

22. See Karl Rahner and Herbert Vorgrimler, *Concise Theological Dictionary*, London 1965, 30–1.

23. Paul Davies, *God and the New Physics*, London 1983, ix; see Stephen Hawking, *a Brief History of Time*, London 1988, 136, 169, 175; John D. Barrow and Frank J. Tipler, *The Anthropic Cosmological Principle*, Oxford 1986, 677.

24. The most thorough study of this material, to which I am much indebted in what follows, is Mary Midgley's Gifford Lectures for 1990: *Science as Salvation. A Modern Myth and its Meaning*, London 1992.

25. *The Anthropic Cosmological Principle*, 658.

26. Rahner, 'The Hermeneutics of Eschatological Assertions' 343.

27. Peter Atkins, *The Creation*, Oxford 1987, 127; William Day, *Genesis on Planet Earth: The Search for Life's Beginning*, East Lansing 1979, 392; Freeman Dyson, 'Time without end: physics and biology in an open universe', *Review of Modern Physics*, Vol. 51, no. 3, 1979, 454, my italics; J. D. Bernal, *The World, the Flesh, and The Devil*, London 1929, 35; Keith Oatley, *Brain Mechanisms and Mind*, New York 1972; for these passages, see Midgley, *Science as Salvation*.

28. Midgley, *Science as Salvation*, 223.

29. Ecclesiastes 1.9.

30. Donald MacKinnon, 'Absolute and Relative in History: A Theological Reflection on the Centenary of Lenin's birth', *Explorations in Theology 5*, London 1979, 59.

31. Ibid., 64, 59 (his italics).

32. Pierre Teilhard de Chardin, 'The Salvation of Mankind', *Science and Christ*, London 1968, 141.

33. Milbank, *Theology and Social Theory*, 1, 6.

34. Ibid., 433; see Hans Urs von Balthasar, *The Glory of the Lord. I. Seeing the Form*, Edinburgh 1982, 680–1; Lash, *Believing Three Ways*, 63.

Pluralism in Theological Truth

John E. Thiel

One way of construing pluralism is to think of it as the very fact of cultural differences, including differences in the intellectual culture of world-views and truth-claims. Now while this construal would not be wrong, it must be regarded as minimalist and only relatively adequate. For given this account, there would be no culture that could not be described as pluralist. Cultures in general evince some awareness of boundaries marking the difference between their own meaningful claims and those of other, often competing, cultures. Moreover, even cultures tied to customary ideas and behaviours provide some room for variety in how their ideas are held and behaviours enacted. The inadequacy of this construal is that it accounts neither for the status that difference or plurality have achieved in the modern period, nor for the effect of pluralism on all dimensions of modern life, including and perhaps especially the very ways in which we make claims to the truth.

As a modern phenomenon, pluralism is best understood as the recognition of the relativity of truth-claims. So perceived, pluralism is first and foremost a perspective on meaning in the face of difference. While a pre-modern mentality tends to see its ways and beliefs as universally valid and so to regard difference as strange or even as false, a modern mentality accepts the historicity of truth-claims within a pluralistic world. Pluralism often leads to the consciousness that the diversity of customs, laws, institutions, morals, religions and commitments one encounters person-ally, societally and globally cannot offer a universal standpoint from which the truth of the many claims and practices can be adjudicated. This consciousness itself, as it takes shape in modern and post-modern ideologies as different as political liberalism, democratic socialism, feminism and deconstructive criticism, encourages the proliferation of truth-claims and thus confirms the mentality in which pluralism emerges.

Even though the history of theology offers a great variety of styles, approaches and methods, it is difficult, then, to speak of pluralism in theology until the modern period, and perhaps only as an accepted part of theological life since the second half of the twentieth century. By now we take for granted that process, narrative, feminist, African-American, Asian, Hispanic, hermeneutical and transcendental (to name a few!) are qualifiers designating particular theological foci and strategies, and evincing a disciplinary pluralism that is rich indeed. But these and other modern and post-modern approaches to theology primarily express the mentality of pluralism, an awareness of the relativity of theology's knowledge among other forms of knowledge and a recognition of the historicity of theology's own truth-claims. As is true of culture in general, the pluralistic mentality on the part of those who share the culture of theology confirms and fosters the proliferation of meaning that has come to characterize the modern history of this discipline.

The traditional self-understandings of theology as the science of divine revelation (Catholicism) or the exegesis of God's revealed Word (Protestantism) have had to reckon with their own qualified status within the pluralism of difference. On the one hand, Christian theology in the modern period has had to come to terms with the claims of other religions, and with the inescapable fact that the historico-critical interpretation of those claims can apply just as well to its own. On the other hand, theology has had to deal with its own internal pluralism, not only in the methodological sub-division of its task into specialist sub-disciplines but also in the form of its proclamation – the very way in which theology makes and argues for its claims to the truth about God, Christ and humanity. This internal pluralism has been of greater consequence for theology than its efforts to face the claims of non-Christian religions. The theological problem of religious pluralism concerns the relationship between Christianity's truth-claims and the truth-claims of other traditions, and can be addressed, at least in principle, by presuming the coherence of theology's traditional claims. The internal pluralism of modern theology, however, challenges the classical understanding of its claims to the truth and introduces the need for the most basic revision of its disciplinary self-understanding.

Traditionally, theology has regarded its time-honoured claims as universal, as expressions of an absolute and saving truth that, in the well-known phrase of Vincent of Lerins, has been believed 'everywhere, always, by all'. Theology's internal pluralism in the modern period, however, reflects the particularized foci and strategies through which its truth is offered to the church and the world. The result is that the claims of modern theology often qualify the conception of universality held throughout the earlier history of the discipline. Indeed, modern theology has often offered its most striking insights into the meaning of the gospel by intentionally eschewing universal portraits of Christian truth, and exploring scripture and tradition instead for more regional truths that speak to very particular questions, problems or experiences. By regional truth-claims I mean beliefs both expressive and formative of particular experiences, circumstances and perspectives, whether these be defined by the specific character of culture, race, gender or even personal experience. Feminist, African-American and Asian theologies come quickly to mind as examples of interpretation committed to the value of regional theological truth. But in their light, even modern approaches to theology that remain committed to a universal presentation of Christian truth – transcendental theologies, for example – show themselves actually to be regional expressions of Christian belief tied to a particular historico-cultural experience, and exhibiting the biases of race, nationality and perhaps even gender.

Does the internal pluralism of modern theology constitute a watershed in the way theological truth-claims are or can be made? Have regional claims to the truth, the inevitable expressions of historical consciousness, superseded the value or even the possibility of universal theological claims? Or can theology continue to make universal claims for the truth while yet embracing the pluralism that characterizes its modern disciplinary commitments? We can begin to consider these questions by exploring the conceptions of universality to which Christianity subscribed throughout its classical period.

Classical conceptions of universality

We can distinguish between two broad conceptions of universality in the Christian tradition that influenced its classical understanding of the nature of theological knowledge: epistemological universality and ecclesial universality.

Epistemological universality reflects the assumption held throughout the Christian tradition (and Western culture largely to our times) that valid knowledge is founded on abstract unities or universals transcending space and time and in which any particular act of knowing – theological or otherwise – participates. Platonism is the most influential expression of this assumption, though Stoicism also shares its values. Through such noetic participation in what Platonists called the super-sensible 'form' or *eidos* or what Stoics called the *logos spermatikos*, knowing achieves a universal character that remains impervious to the spatio-temporal character of sensible experience. The Judaeo-Christian doctrine of creation complements this epistemological universality by espousing a holistic view of reality in which God is both the source of being and, with the divine ideas now substituting for Platonic or Stoic versions of the noetic ideal, the goal of intellectual striving. To the degree that classical theology claims God as the direct object of its epistemic endeavours, the universal character of its knowledge is all the more presumed.

Ecclesial universality reflects the belief present in the tradition from the early Christian centuries that the truth of the church is 'catholic'. This belief, a profession of faith deemed worthy of inclusion in the ancient creeds, advances the epistemological assumptions described above. The truth of the church is universal because it lies in the mystery of a God unbounded by space and time. But it is also important to note the spatio-temporal character of this ecclesial mark. The universality of the church achieves expression principally in ecclesial doctrine – what the members of the church believe in their hearts and enact through their wills from time to time and place to place. Affirmations of the universality of the church's teaching set ecclesial faith in a global perspective defined temporally by the continuity of faith joining each successive generation of believers and spatially by the geographical extension of ecclesial boundaries. The mission of the church to spread the gospel to all nations is supported by this spatio-temporal conception of universality succinctly expressed in the Vincentian maxim cited earlier. To the degree that theology is a discipline in the service of the church, its classical task was set by its responsibility to represent and to promulgate the universality of the church through its own truth-claims.

These conceptions of universality have been subject to fundamental revision in the modern period. Indeed, in the case of epistemological universality little remains of the ancient position. Post-Hegelian philosophy has called into question the classical tradition of Christian metaphysics, especially its epistemological assumption that ahistorical universals, including the universality of the divine existence, constitute the proper objects of knowing. Epistemologies in the hermeneutical trajectory of Heidegger, Gadamer and Ricoeur are historical in orientation, assuming that what counts as truth is significantly a product of cultural experience. Epistemologies in the radical historicist trajectory of Nietzsche, Foucault and Derrida push this historical orientation to the rejection of overarching meaning, purposiveness and universality in epistemic results. Whether revisionist or radical in perspective, these epistemologies see acts of knowing as regional in their conduct, object and claims.

This regional or contextualized approach to epistemology has been the explicit agenda of various types of twentieth-century philosophy which, broadly-speaking, can be described as non-foundationalist. Following in the steps of Peirce, James and Dewey, contemporary American pragmatists like Willard Van Orman Quine, Richard Rorty, and Donald Davidson have advanced nuanced philosophical arguments against Platonic, and especially Cartesian, epistemologies, which they judge to be foundationalist. Foundationalist epistemologies, they argue, posit some first principle that serves as a 'foundation' for the entire edifice of knowledge. Whether the foundations of knowing take the form of Descartes's clear and distinct ideas, the givenness of sense experience for Locke, or Kant's transcendental categories of the understanding, they are invoked as immediately justified beliefs the certainty of which is basic to the large body of knowledge and justifies its claims. Foundations of knowing, by their very nature, are posited as universal authenticators of truth-claims. They exist, their defenders maintain, as the very conditions of knowing. As non-inferential truth, the foundations of knowledge provide a point of departure for logical deduction or a foothold for the tentative climb of thinking by way of inference towards valid knowledge.

For the pragmatists named above, foundationalist epistemologies are woefully inadequate. The fact that different sorts of foundations for knowledge – both chthonic and ethereal – have posed in the history of philosophy as immediately experienced certainties itself deconstructs the foundationalist claim. In the face of this anomaly, any epistemic foundation shows itself to be the product of a philosopher's blind faith, an expression of the vain hope that the business of justifying our beliefs can be concluded in a universally accessible and doubt-free truth. As Rorty suggests, foundationalism is a type of fundamentalism in which truths are 'certain because of their causes rather than because of the arguments given for them'.[1] For non-foundationalist philosophers, there is no evidence in experience or knowledge that foundational, universal causes for knowing exist. Our knowledge is holistic. To use Quine's metaphor, its claims are an intricate web of mutually related, foundationless beliefs that our arguments sustain, revise or delete.[2] Its truth is not fixed and final, but relative and ever in process. A natural consequence of this stance, which has largely become axiomatic among contemporary philosophers, is that truth-claims possess not a universal but a regional value. Meaning flourishes only in specific contexts defined by such variables as background beliefs, language and use. In this non-foundationalist perspective, knowledge is tied to co-ordinate systems of our own making whose infinite particularities dash the universality to which the classical philosophical tradition aspired.

Since the conception of ecclesial universality reflects the assumptions of epistemological universality, non-foundationalist criticism clearly has important implications for our understanding of the church as catholic. Moreover, the spatio-temporal variety of ecclesial universality finds itself at least in need of revision as recent criticism makes us aware of its own limitations, and as the increasingly louder voices of regionalism are heard in the church. Edward Farley, for example, describes the tendency to distortion inherent in the traditional conception of ecclesial universality by noting the extent to which the mark of catholicity is all too often absolutized in the history of human sin.[3] In terms of the dimension of space, this distortion occurs as a particular place – its culture, customs and values – is declared globally normative for the expression and practice of the faith. In terms of the dimension of time, this false absolutizing occurs as a particular ecclesial moment – its world-view, assumptions and language – is declared resistant to interpretation and fixed as normative for all later times. In both instances, the universal is but a pretence through which the regional seeks power by masking the particularity of its claims.

Along the same lines, recent developments in the church's understanding of its mission to evangelize chart subtle revisions in the traditional spatio-temporal view of its catholicity. Paul Lakeland has noted that prior to Vatican II the church understood itself as an institution orientated on success.[4] In this model, missionary achievement is conceived as the winning and retention of converts throughout the world. This strategic conception of spatio-temporal universality was not emphasized in the documents of Vatican II, which, by developing an ecclesiology with communitarian emphases, paved the way for local, dialogical perspectives on the mission of the church, such as those exhibited by the base Christian communities of Latin America and a growing regional awareness of the reception of the faith. Furthermore, the Council's appreciation of the truth of other religious traditions in *Nostra Aetate*[5] promulgated the ecclesiology of the Council by qualifying a traditional conception of spatio-temporal universality which simply identified catholicity with the institutional church. This appreciation in turn encouraged a greater sensitivity in the theology of missions to the issue of inculturation, the challenge of preaching the gospel meaningfully in particular cultural contexts.

These shifts in the epistemological and ecclesial conceptions of universality can be ascribed to the advent of pluralism in the logic of epistemology and in the faith of the church. In time-honoured, Anselmian, fashion, as well as in its most formal configuration, theology is faith seeking understanding. It is a discipline that expounds ecclesial faith by appealing to the canons of ordered thinking prescribed by philosophy. On both of these counts, faith and logic, theology faces the pluralism of historical consciousness, and the implications of this pluralism for its claims to the truth.

Pluralism in theology and the dilemma of universal truth

Since the epistemological conclusions of our best philosophers and undeniable developments in our ecclesiology suggest that the truth of the mind and the heart flourishes in the particularities of our lives and the ways they are lived with others, how can our truth-claims be more than particular? This question is not troublesome for the non-foundational philosophers considered above, who are happy to relinquish universal conceptions of truth and often prefer to speak of valued claims as *meaning*ful rather than as *truth*ful, lest terminology itself unwittingly serve as a Trojan horse for foundationalist assumptions. Nor is it troublesome for social scientists, whose disciplines were born as historicist attempts to explain the new pluralism. Theologians, however, practise an ancient discipline devoted to the interpretation of a universal revelation for the sake of a universal church, which nevertheless, in its distinctively modern practice, for the sake of its own intelligibility, cannot simply ignore the criticism of universal claims considered above. Some historical observations will introduce our efforts to respond constructively to this difficulty.

By the early nineteenth century, theologians began to speak of human experience as a discrete source of theological knowledge. This represented a change in practice from pre-modern theologians who understood scripture and tradition (Catholic) or scripture alone (Protestant) to be the sole authoritative sources of theology. This is not to say, of course, that classical theologians did not invoke experience, theirs and others, in theological reflection. However, they did not understand experience to be a particular, truthful resource to which adequate theological reflection had to be faithful. In spite of often formidable opposition (especially on the part of Roman Catholic neo-scholasticism and the anti-Modernist movement), modern theologians cultivated this assumption to the point that it became axiomatic for the practice of their discipline.[6]

Throughout most of the past two centuries, theologians have been inclined to speak of the experiential source of theology as universal, as tied in some way to the conditions of human experience or to the most general experience of the church. Schleiermacher's feeling of absolute dependence, Rahner's pre-thematic experience of holy mystery, and descriptions of the *sensus fidei* from Newman to Vatican II's *Lumen Gentium* all serve as examples. But the very fact that experience, as a matter of course, began to be treated as one of the truthful sources of theology meant that its own character could be referenced in how it was authoritatively invoked. While there is no shortage of those in human history who have argued or believed that there are universal dimensions of experience, experience is undeniably, and indeed most dramatically, particular, both in the manner in which it is encountered subjectively and in the manner in which we measure its meaningfulness for our lives. As theologians made this particularity a value in their interpretations of scripture and tradition, the result was more particularized theological truth-claims, and even the birth of critical theological genres – feminist, Asian, Hispanic, African-American, for example – devoted to their explicit exposition. Modern theological pluralism, then, is a function of the belief that regional experiences have truths to tell that focus the Christian message, and that along with scripture and tradition are theologically normative.

These particularized theological claims often stand in uncomfortable relationship to claims on behalf of ecclesial universality, or to theological styles, both pre-modern and modern, that are universal in orientation. Regional theologies find that particular events and situations in the lives of particular peoples embody both the reality of sin and the liberating power of God's grace, and insist that theological truth be measured by the use to which it is put in circumstances calling for Christian praxis. From their contextualized standpoint, regional theologies fear that uncritical appeals to universal experience or to the church's traditional claims to catholicity too readily ignore the historical, cultural and existential particularities which shape how the gospel is interpreted, preached and enacted. They are suspicious of exclusively theoretical approaches to theology which take their point of departure from claims purporting to be the experience of all, but which may in fact only be the experience of a few. Regional theologies, then, not only offer constructive interpretations of the meaning of scripture and tradition for contemporary Christian life but also see their task as the criticism of theological claims to universality which are only particular, albeit powerful, representations of ecclesial meaning.

And yet, regional theologies by no means deny in principle the claim to catholicity articulated in the church's basic credal beliefs. To do so would reduce Christian faith to experiences too particular to be true to the gospel's promise of salvation, and its theological interpretation to judgments that could as easily be rendered by value-orientated applications of the social sciences. Regional theologies faithful to the Christian tradition understand their criticism of spurious claims to universality to promulgate that very tradition as a legitimate development of its teaching. They do not understand the value of regional truths to lie in their narrowness but in their capacity to reveal the breadth of the human encounter with God in the life of the church.

Here we meet what we might call the dilemma of universality, a dilemma posed by the very character of modern theology. On the one hand, the inclusion of experience among the sources of theology allowed the truth of regional experiences to achieve a degree of normativeness for theology that they did not possess on classical assumptions. This development was responsible for a pluralism in the proclamation of theology, as regional interpretations of the Christian message reflected the particularities of human experience and its claims to truth. This proclamatory pluralism, exhibited taxonomically in the rise of diverse critical approaches to theology in this last part of our century, in turn exposed the regional commitments of theologies which purported to be universal in approach. On the other hand, even theology aware of and valuing the regionality of its claims cannot shrink from its commitment to universal truth, lest it relinquish the very claims of scripture and tradition by which Christian faith abides. This dilemma continues to vex the practice of modern theology, its particularist and universalist poles defining the interests of divided theological camps or authoritative ministries, each suspicious of the other's commitments.

The regional character of universal claims

As a theological problem, the dilemma of universality exhibits all the markings of an insoluble dialectical puzzle. Like the philosophical conundrum of the one and the many, it takes shape as mutually defined limit-concepts each claim a priority immediately shaken by the claim of its opposite, yet each requiring the value of the other for its own intelligibility. Although this problem is a recent arrival in the history of theology, it shows signs of being a perennial one to which, it would seem, theologians should simply resign themselves. While this dilemma will never yield a clear answer to the question of the proper practice of theology, its exploration will allow us to struggle, perhaps even productively, with the issues of authority and normativeness in theological interpretation.

As has been noted above, Christian believers make universal truth-claims as a matter of their very faith and practice. Theological reflection on that faith and practice, then, in whatever style we might find it, would contradict itself were it to maintain that only regional, and not universal, truth-claims were authoritative – an abiding fear of those who assume that theology is properly the reiteration of scripture or doctrine. Regional theologies presuppose such universal truth-claims, whether expressed in scripture, doctrine or personal confession, as background beliefs for the more particular insights they have to offer on their content. Even the critical regard in which regional theologies hold universal claims properly is governed by their search for a more authentic catholicity, one that is able to embrace the particular concerns highlighted in their theological formulations. While non-foundational philosophical sensibilities might reject the notion of universal truth as a groundless fantasy, a regional, contextually-oriented theology could not, since the universal truth-claims of scripture and tradition stand among the particularities of its own commitments. This epistemic irony, that Christian particularity involves the assertion of universal claims, reflects the most basic character of Christian faith itself. Taken as a canon of theological interpretation, this irony in its own way accords rather well with the contextual orientation of a non-foundational account of knowledge.

This contextual perspective on truth-claims in turn enables one to see the regional dimensions of the universal tradition that theology holds as authoritative. The universality of the tradition remains inextricably bound to a host of regional stances, not merely in the sense that a tradition encompasses particularities as the whole does its parts but in the more fundamental respect that what we affirm as a tradition is a valued perspective on what were originally regional truth-claims. The truth-claims of the universal tradition are, to use a visual metaphor, the expressions of faith in retrospect. Their universality as Christian truth is only visible from the standpoint of present Christian commitments looking back on the past, judging their continuity with the commitments of past believers, and including that judgment among the articles of faith. Prior to their retrospective inclusion among the articles of faith, these claims to Christian universality were first regional. The Gospel of John, for example, originally expressed the faith of a Christian community at odds in its belief with other Christian communities. However imperial its atmosphere, Nicaea was only a local council to the bishops in attendance. The thirteenth-century theologian Peter Olivi made questionable arguments in support of the doctrine of papal infallibility that later proved influential in the nineteenth-century declaration of the dogma. Such a historical description of the workings of tradition in no way diminishes the value of its universal claims for the church. Its advantage lies in showing the extent to which the universal truths of the tradition achieve their status inductively.

Acknowledging the productive role of regional truths in the church's universal tradition has important implications for contemporary theology.

To say that theology is responsible to the universal truth of the Christian tradition also means that theology is responsible to claims originally regional in scope which in faith were seen to possess a greater worth for a greater number of believers. The regionality of such claims may have been eclipsed in pre-modern times by an uncritical understanding of epistemological and ecclesial universality in which regional verities remained obscured and unable to achieve a distinction of their own. The qualified authority modern theology accords to experience, however, allows regional truth-claims to stand out in relief and to be appreciated for their contribution to the Christian vision both in the received tradition and in the ongoing task of theology of bringing clarity to faith. A consequence of this recognition is that all members of the church have the responsibility to discern such truths and to be receptive to their claims as potentially authentic propagations of the gospel. Theologians have the added responsibility of featuring such truths in theological investigations that bring new insights to the church's universal tradition.

Another reason to value regional truth-claims theologically is implicit in our analysis of tradition. If the ecclesial past demonstrates that in time some regional truths come to universal esteem, then the regional truth of our own time, especially as offered in theological presentation, might very well be deemed the truth of the universal tradition in a time yet to come. This potential in any regional claim does not mean that such claims are theologically privileged because of how they may one day be judged. Regional claims potentially possess theological authority in principle, and not as a matter of fact. But this potential in regional claims certainly means that theologies broader in the scope of their claims are not exclusively privileged simply because they more directly represent what is now the universal tradition.

By the same token, regional theological claims do not possess warrant only in their capacity to become larger in scope than they presently are. Regional truth-claims may have authority in their own right, even if they never come to be ranked among the tradition's universal truths. When offered as descriptions of the absences or systematic distortions in the tradition – the judgment of Juan Luis Segundo, for example, that there is an ecclesial tendency to absolutize the dogmatic tradition or the judgment of Rosemary Radford Ruether that all theological categories of the major Christian traditions have been distorted by androcentrism[7] – regional truth-claims are made in a critical mode that, as such, could not develop towards inclusion in the universal tradition. Regional theological claims of this sort involve a negative hermeneutics that require their critical distance from the universal tradition, however sympathetically they may finally assess its authentic dimensions. Their veridical worth is contrapuntal, a posture that easily leads to their being misunderstood as secular criticism devoid of commitment. Such negative judgments, though, often express a prophetic faith crucially important for understanding the universal tradition, identifying pretenders to its truth, and prompting its meaningful development.

Toward a non-foundational understanding of tradition

The pluralism of modern theology in the very manner of its claims to the truth may be a confusing and even unsettling fact of contemporary ecclesial life, especially for a tradition accustomed to measuring authentic catholicity by the unanimity engendered by its claims. But it also presents an opportunity for theology to be representative of the different experiences, hopes and visions of the church it serves, as well as responsive to the expectations of postmodern epistemologies. As regional truth-claims have come to be distinguished in the modern period from their universal counterparts, they have achieved an integrity, and even an authority, of their own. Perhaps the newness of this circumstance for an ancient discipline explains why regional truth-claims meet with suspicion on the part of those accustomed to understanding theological responsibility as the uncritical representation of the universal tradition.

Recognizing the regional character of universal truth-claims enhances one's appreciation for the complex mutuality of regional and universal truth-claims, and so for what we might call the non-foundational character of the Christian tradition that theology holds normative. In such a conceptualization, the authoritative tradition is not identified exclusively with beliefs regarded as universal in scope, nor is the inevitable problem of priority within that tradition faced by suggesting a hierarchy of truths whose exclusive universality is still presumed. Recent philosophical criticism helps us to understand the degree to which Platonic or even Cartesian understandings of ecclesial tradition are prone to foundationalist distortions in which a certain expression of a dogma, belief or magisterial teaching is regarded as determinative of the meaning of the tradition. By this reductionism in the logic of faith, the tradition's claims to catholicity ironically become parochial. A non-foundational conception of tradition would regard the universal and regional dimensions of Christian truth as a single web of belief in which catholic and particular claims are mutually constitutive, mutually revisable, and expressive of the church's pluralism through time and culture. A non-foundational understanding of tradition might very well distinguish between stronger and weaker filaments in the web of belief or between tighter or looser weavings in its elaborate organization. But it would not expect a single strand of the web to hold the others in place. Nor, to continue the analogy, would it expect the authority of universal Christian claims alone to establish the web's integrity. A theology responsible to the Christian tradition so conceived would value the authority of both universal and regional claims to the truth, and thus embrace, in Christian terms, a modern pluralism that otherwise seems only threatening.

Notes

1. Richard Rorty, *Philosophy and the Mirror of Nature*, Princeton, NJ 1979, 157.

2. W. V. Quine, 'On Empirically Equivalent Systems of the World', *Erkenntnis* 9, 1975, 313; W. V. Quine and J. S. Ullian, *The Web of Belief*, New York 1970.

3. Edward Farley, *Ecclesial Reflection: An Anatomy of Theological Method*, Philadelphia 1982, 230–6.

4. Paul Lakeland, *Theology and Critical Theory: The Discourse of the Church*, Nashville, TN, 195f.

5. 'Declaration on the Relation of the Church to Non-Christian Religions' (*Nostra Aetate*, 2), in *Vatican II: The Conciliar and Postconciliar Documents*, ed. A. Flannery, Northport, NY 1987, 739.

6. For a full discussion of these issues, see John E. Thiel, *Imagination and Authority: Theological Authorship in the Modern Tradition*, Minneapolis, MN 1991.

7. Juan Luis Segundo, *The Liberation of Theology*, Dublin 1977, 180–1; Rosemary Radford Ruether, *Sexism and God-Talk: Toward a Feminist Theology*, Boston and London 1983, 37.

The Problem of Universality and Inculturation with Regard to Patterns of Theological Thinking

Aloysius Pieris

Apprehensions about the theme

The theme of this article has been formulated for me by the editors in the key words contained in the title. But this theme, as well as its formulation, is fraught with many methodological difficulties which I have discussed at length elsewhere.[1] In brief, they are as follows:

1. The very word 'inculturation' presupposes a theory of culture and religion which certain forms of emergent Asian theologies reject as a misconception of the Asian reality and an anachronistic imposition of a first-century Mediterranean experience on contemporary Asia.

2. Besides, the phrase 'inculturation of theology [or of liturgy]' presupposes a concept of universal theology [or a universal liturgy] that exists by itself in a non-inculturated form waiting to be particularized in a given context.

3. Furthermore, the first initiators of inculturation had misconceived their own theology, ecclesiology, liturgy and (now christology), as something universal to be inculturated, thus giving fuel to the charge of Euro-ecclesiastical imperialism.

4. Finally, there is also the great unfinished debate about the real or apparent antagonism between inculturation and liberation, and a well-founded fear among liberationalists that the inculturationist model is advertised and advocated by certain interested parties whose secret agenda is to thwart the march of liberation theologies.

Aware of these difficulties, I shall evaluate the current theological scene from the cultural perspective I know best.

The Indic cultural context

The Indic culture in which I live my received faith in Christ entices me to evaluate my equally received theology in terms of the dialectics between theory and praxis (*vidyā-carana*), between a view of life and a way of life (*darśana-pratipadā*), between the salvific Reality and its moral imperative (*dharma-vinaya*), between the sovereign truth and the sovereign path which include each other (*āryasatya-āryamārga*); and so on.

Now, this manner of perceiving soteriology as a mutually inclusive dyad of 'seeing and doing' imparts its dialectical character to the task of 'speaking' about that which is at once 'seen as the ultimate truth' and 'sought as the ultimate goal'. The basic ingredients of theology are seeing, doing and speaking. Religious discourse is speech prompted by the perception of a truth-goal and marked by the struggle to arrive at it. All other speech is purely speculative and soteriologically inconsequential.

Christian 'theo-logy', seen from this perspective, seems to be a religious discourse (*logos*) addressed to, by and regarding *theos*, who is both the ultimate truth and the ultimate goal. It is a systematic discourse and a disciplined speech commensurate with that truth-goal. This discourse (*logos*), no doubt, is inherent in the very reality of the truth-goal (*theos*). This is the basic axiom on which Christian theology is founded.

The constitutive dimension of the Christian discourse

The question of theology as discourse in the Christian context presupposes the following datum of faith: that the truth-goal is identified as the unspeakable One (*theos*/God) who becomes speakable only as the speech (*logos*) uttered by the unspoken speaker (*pneuma*/Spirit). The Spirit is the subject, not the object of discourse. All discourse about the unspeakable One is the revelatory word uttered by the unspoken speaker.

Furthermore, this speech is also the medium by which *theos*, our source of salvation, becomes accessible to us. To put it more clearly, the word of revelation is also the medium of salvation and the path to intimacy with the Ultimate. Thus all theology revolves round this word-medium-path; it alone is speakable and therefore spoken. Being speech, it is theology itself, seminally.

This word-medium-path has been available to all tribes, races and peoples of all times and all places. It has been recognized by various names (*Dharma, Mārga, Tao*, etc.), giving rise to many forms of discourse.[2] It is too profound to be exhausted by one single utterance – be it our human utterance, or even that of the unspeakable One. For both these utterances –

the human and the divine – are emitted by the breath of the same unspoken speaker who speaks in God and in people or, more accurately, in non-persons covenanted with God.

Three theological patterns

But the belief that Jesus of Nazareth is *the* enfleshed historical manifestation of this word-medium-path turns Christian theology into a christology. Such naming, however, is not a condition for salvation demanded by the Word which, being universal, operates even among those who do not recognize it by that name. It is the word-medium-path that saves, not the name one gives to it. Naming which belongs to theology cannot be universal.

Now, the theandric speech recognized as 'Jesus' by Christians is not merely an explanatory word (*logos*), but also one that is creative (*dabar*) and directional (*hodos*). For the breath by which it is voiced is the Spirit of wisdom, the Spirit of love and the Spirit that blows all words towards the mystery of ultimate silence.

Regrettably, therefore, Christian theology has sinned against the Spirit by dividing her discourse into three separate theological idioms. For want of better terms, let them be known as the *logos* model, the *dabar* model and the *hodos* model of theology.

Logos model: philosophical or scholastic theology

Logos is reason and rationality. If we prescind from the Johannine synthesis of *logos* and *dabar* – something rare in current theological thinking – we are left with a theology that insists on the all-pervasive role of intelligibility. Jesus of Nazareth is primary explanation of God and creation. He is the one who makes sense of what is otherwise meaningless.

In this view, salvation is knowledge of God; theology is the explanation of revelation. 'I believe that I may understand' (*credo ut intelligam*). My mind must satisfy itself in understanding God with the help of revelation. Faith is a gift of knowledge that allows the intellect to give its assent (*assensus intellectus*) to truth(s) explained by those who have received the divine guarantee to teach such truth.

Love results from knowledge. Knowledge may culminate in love, but that love is affective knowledge. The final salvation is a beatific vision enjoyed by the human mind elevated to the new level of understanding. Contemplation of the mystery of God is the goal of Christian existence; action (both social action of an 'ethical' order and ascetical practices of a 'spiritual' order) is a stepping stone to that goal. The anticipation of this final salvation here on earth is infused knowledge which contemplation is.

Theoretically speaking, even obedience (i.e., action in conformity with the Word) comes after an understanding of the Word. In theory, therefore, the government (*imperium*) of a Jesus-community belongs to the domain of the intellect. When the community learns collectively the will of God, it is moved to obey it. The will follows the intellect (*voluntas sequitur intellectum*). This is how St Thomas understood obedience.[3] He represents the noblest moment of the *logos* movement before it was overtaken by the decadent scholasticism of later centuries. For, in the decadent form, an emphasis on knowledge that generates power seems to have vitiated community-government into a one-party rule. The following three observations are, therefore, relevant:

1. Rightness and the wrongness in the formulation of truth is crucial to this theology. Dogma-heresy dialectics play an important role in maintaining the purity of truth. Authority is the result of possessing truth rather than of being possessed by truth. The power to rule is associated with the privilege of knowing the truth. An infallible authority guarantees the possibility of such knowledge for all. The Word of God may be, theoretically, above the teaching authority in the church (*Verbum Dei*, no. 9), but in practice it has to be interpreted as the true Word by that infallible authority. For there is a magisterium which has the power to interpret the Word and demand assent to *that* Word as interpreted by it.

2. The word-medium is believed to be entrusted to knowledgeable persons. In their consecrated hands and in their hallowed mouths, this word can be a medium of transformation or transubstantiation. The sacraments are speech uttered by these privileged persons, rather than speech of the unspoken speaker. In Greek Orthodox theology, on the contrary, the transformation (*metabole*) is rightly regarded as an *epiclesis*, that is, a 'manifestation [of the transformed matter] by the Spirit'; but, here, in *logos* theology, such change of species is 'caused' by the 'words of institution' uttered by the aforementioned persons.[4]

3. The liturgy is so organized as to exhibit this power-principle operating in the church. A eucharist revolves around this person, with special dress (and in some cases with a special headgear and a wand of authority). Such persons preside over the ceremonies, where the eucharistic species as well as the community seem to be under their control. The Word is not the focus of the celebration. The cleric who handles the Word is the one who dominates the liturgy. At his words, the species change; God's people bend their knees, and receive what he confects for them. The eucharist as celebrated according to this theology is the

symbol of how the power of knowing the Word exercises power even over the Word.

Such is *logos* which is not *dabar*.

The *dabar* model: liberation theology

The *dabar* pattern of theology moves in another direction altogether. The word-medium is not merely a speech that displays authoritative knowledge, but an utterance that creates and transforms. The theological task is not just to 'interpret' the world philosophically but to 'change' it.

Speech, in this case, is not a rational explanation but a happening, an event. Here, therefore, history and revelation meet. The word of salvation is continually heard in history – not only in the history of Israel and of Jesus, but in the continuing history of the world. *Extra historiam nulla salus*. To obey the Word is to partake in the *epiclesis*, to share in the Spirit's work of manifesting, here and now, a transformed world.

Hearing the Word does not primarily coincide with understanding it; rather, the Word heard is the Word obeyed. It is the execution of the Word that brings understanding of the Word. Praxis is the first formulation of theory. *Doing* the truth leads to discerning the Path – a procedure that would sound incongruous in *logos* theology.

Hence there can be no authority above the Word. The one who is faithful to the Word – the prophet – is the one who has authority to announce it. The Word shows its power in the prophet; the prophet has no power over the Word. Kerygma has priority over the cult. The Prophet's word is prefaced by 'It is the Lord who says'. It is not a given infallibility that guarantees his or her credibility, but the transforming effect of the Word visibly evident in the prophet's life (personal witness) and in other readable signs of human wholeness by which the prophet anticipates the new order (miracles of healing). The Word announced is the Word attested, in this twofold manner. Hence prophetic authority is not magisterial (in the sense in which the word 'magisterium' has developed in the *logos* stream of theology) but martyrial.

All prophets – from the First Testament prophets beginning with Moses, down to Jesus and his precursor in the Second Testament – were persons who entered the history of their people at the risk of courting dangerous social conflicts which in many cases culminated in premature death. After Jesus, the cross has now become the symbol of this social conflict and the final proof of martyrial authority, for it is on the cross that the Word triumphs, both as revelatory and salvific; it is there that prophetic authority is finally vindicated.

In various liberation theologies, this active participation in the transformation of history through the *via crucis* constitutes the *fons et culmen*
(the source and summit) of Christian life – in contrast with the Second
Vatican Council's emphasis on the liturgical celebrations as the source and
summit (of a historical struggle). The paschal mystery is primarily enacted
in the socio-historical context of the liturgy of life. This means that 'formal
prayer' – both as private devotion and as communal worship – is,
respectively, a personal interiorization and an ecclesial celebration of the
liturgy of life. This shift of emphasis illustrates the difference between the
logos model and the *dabar* model of Christian theology.

The *hodos* model: theology as search for wholeness

The word-medium in this stream of theological thought is essentially a
path, a process, a journey. It could be viewed as an ascent to a mountain, or
a descent to the depths of the mystery; or perhaps an inward journey
towards the interior of one's own castle. Sometimes it is described as a
series of steps leading to a summit (*scala perfectionum*). Accordingly, the
pilgrims could be categorized in terms of their position in the path:
incipientes, *proficientes*, *perfecti*. The trajectory is itself designated
progressively as the purgative, the illuminative and the unitive way.

The God-experience expressing itself in God-talk appears to be a
graduated path in which 'moral life' is the first phase leading to 'spiritual
life' which, in its turn, is once more seen as two stages: the 'ascetic' stage
where one's personal effort to move towards the goal is registered intensely
in the soul; and the 'mystical' stage when the magnetic pull of the goal is so
overwhelming as to minimize the gravitational drag of the early ascesis.

This way of considering morality as the necessary minimum and
spirituality as an ascent towards a higher stage (counsels of perfection?),
and of dividing spirituality itself into a lower form of active struggle and a
higher form of passive absorption, is typical of a *hodos* theology that
identifies the goal of the path as 'perfection in formal prayer'.[5] This manner
of defining spirituality tallies with the *logos* theology, according to which
action is transcended by mystical knowledge gained through formal
prayer.

Another school understands spirituality in terms of a struggle to bring
God's reign on earth through apostolic labour, that is to say, through an
effort to transform the world socio-spiritually in response to God's will.[6]
This spirituality, which proliferated from the sixteenth century onwards,
speaks in an idiom that is not quite consonant with *logos* theology. But, as
Lozano seems to insinuate, the authentic Christian tradition is one in

which the goal of the spiritual path ought to be what he calls apostolic mysticism.[7] The newly emerging *dabar* theology seems to have an inner affinity with this 'activist' model of *hodos* theology.

Whatever the conflict between the two trends, one thing is clear: the path, once taken, becomes less and less the focus as the journey progresses; the goal becomes the all-pervading concern. Thus, Teresa of Avila seems to have wondered why Jesus the man tends to disappear in the process of her gradual union with God. Merton suggests the answer: Jesus is not the goal but only the way to it.[8] To be one with Christ is to be fully in the path, and therefore goal-consciousness must gradually supersede the path-consciousness.

In the body of the *Exercises*, Ignatius of Loyola, too, is quite insistent on the role of Jesus as the way to be followed, but ceases to mention him in the climactic contemplation of union with God. This is, presumably, because Christ is the medium with which one becomes identified in the course of the journey; thus, through Christ, with Christ and in Christ, the exercitant stands face to face with God, the Father-Mother-Lover-Friend-Coworker. The *hodos* theology scrupulously safeguards the mediational character of Christ.

This is *a fortiori* true of the church and its institutions, which serve as guide posts and pilgrims' rests that one must leave behind as one moves along the path. Hence, there could be (as there have been in the past) conflicts between the practitioners of a *hodos* theology (mystics) and the cultic magisterium that has its roots in a *logos* theology.

A (particular) theology as *the* (universal) theology?

Yves Congar has cited the Ignatian Exercises (no. 363) and other works of that period such as Juan Mair's to demonstrate that there were two theologies in vogue even as late as the beginning of the modern period: 'positive theology' which reflected the affective spirituality of the Fathers, and 'scholastic theology' which was an intellectual and apologetical affirmation of the Catholic doctrines against the heretics.[9] These two correspond to the *hodos* and *logos* models we are talking about here.

It would seem that certain monastic [i.e. positive] theologies such as the Antiochean version taught in the Congregazione Casinese could not survive the Council of Trent.[10] After Trent, *logos* theology dominated the Western patriarchate within the framework of the Latin jurisprudential scheme of guilt and justification.

Jean Leclerq tried his best to retrieve from oblivion the much forgotten monastic theology[11] which was certainly a *hodos* (i.e., positive) theology.

In the Jesuit Constitutions, Ignatius, too, insisted that positive theology should be taught over and above the scholastic type.[12] But the Jesuits, in their preoccupation with apologetics, tilted heavily towards scholasticism and ended up with highly speculative theological pursuits at the turn of the nineteenth century. With that deviation, the *Spiritual Exercises* too became highly intellectualized.[13] It is in this century, thanks to five decades of research, that the theology of the *Exercises* has been rediscovered as a positive theology.

With regard to a reintegration of *dabar* theology, however, we are still very backward. It had been abandoned since the time Christianity was 'inculturated' in the Greco-Roman world. It yet has to be re-absorbed into the mainstream. The contrary idea that the *dabar* model needs the supplementary support of a strong intellectual *logos* theology has been worked out into a persuasive thesis, strongly emphasizing the West's literary tradition in which 'the Word has become Spirit' in the scientific study of texts.[14]

Hence this word of caution about the 'power-generating knowledge' which results from a *logos*-minus-*dabar* development of thought; it manifests itself both in the secular domain with its scientism and technocracy, and in the religious (Christian) world where cultic control coincides with 'the power of knowledge'. A white-robed clerical elite operating in scientific laboratories and in religious sanctuaries amply testify to the effects of a neo-Gnosticism derived from a *logos*-current of knowledge that has been divorced from the *dabar*-stream of loving action.[15] Could Peukert's Habermas-based 'Theology of Communicative Action'[16] be interpreted as an (unconscious ?) attempt at restoring the *dabar* dimension of Christian discourse within the traditional logos theology, even though this terminology is conspicuously absent in his exposition?

Inculturation and liberation

The metacosmic religions of non-semitic Asia seem to follow a twofold trend, like Western Christianity. On the one hand, there is a *hodos* model of religious thought and practice reflecting the mutuality between truth and the path. This tradition has its personal embodiment in the figure of the sage, the guru, the mystic, and is available today in the ashrams or their equivalents. On the other hand, Hinduism, Jainism and Buddhism have also produced a highly speculative brand of scholasticism thanks to centuries of sectarian debates.

It is not surprising, therefore, that the Asian spirituality of the Christian ashrams resonate with the *hodos* stream of Western Christianity, just as Christian intellectuals who have been nourished by the *logos* theology have tried to construct an Asian theology using Hindu-Buddhist philosophical speculation.

This twofold trend in 'inculturation' is in conflict with 'liberation' theologies such as the Minjung theology in Korea, the Dalit theology in India and Asian feminist theology in general, which have their roots in the cosmic religiosity of Asia. These theologies reject the inculturationism of the ashramic and the philosophical models as anti-liberational.[17] For the Asian liberation theologies, unlike these two 'inculturated' versions, have appropriated the *dabar* idiom of the Semitic tradition of Asia. Herein lies the conflict between inculturationists and liberationists.

This conflict cannot, therefore, be resolved until a comprehensive and holistic approach is adopted in Christian discourse. An all-embracing christology (call it universal if you like) is one that weaves together all the three aspects of Christian discourse: Jesus as the word that interprets reality, the medium that transforms history, and the way that leads to the cessation of all discourse.

Notes

1. Aloysius Pieris, *An Asian Theology of Liberation*, Maryknoll 1988, 37–42, 44–5, 51–8, 109–10 etc.; and also in my recent article 'Inculturation: Some Critical Comments', *Vidyajyoti Journal of Theological Reflection*, LVII/11, November 1993, 641–51.

2. See Chapter 10 of my *Love Meets Wisdom. A Christian Experience of Buddhism*, Maryknoll 1989, especially 131–5. See also *An Asian Theology of Liberation* (n. 1), 62–3.

3. As explained in Herbert McCabe, OP, 'Obedience', *New Blackfriars*, June 1984, 280–6.

4. See Alexander Schmemann, *The World a Sacrament*, London 1965, 52–3.

5. By 'formal prayer' is meant the type of prayer which is characterized by a special method and structure, a regularity in time and a definite place. See Giacomo Lercaro, *Methods of Mental Prayer*, London 1957, 1ff.

6. Thus in the *Spiritual Exercises*, no. 189, Ignatius of Loyola insists that conformity with the will of God is the measure of progress in the spiritual path. Hence the various spiritual exercises (which include formal prayer) are mere means of acquiring indifference, i.e. a detachment from one's own selfish pursuits, a discerning mind which alone is capable of discovering God's will, and a willing heart to embrace it. Ignatius defines the *Exercises*, not as a school of prayer, but as a spiritual gymnasium wherein one trains oneself to undertake apostolic labour, i.e., get involved in the work of God's reign.

7. John M. Lozano, 'The Theology and Spirituality of the Apostolic Life', in J. M. Lozano et al., *Ministerial Spirituality and Religious Life*, Chicago 1988, 35ff.

8. See Thomas Merton, 'The Humanity of Christ in Monastic Prayer', *Monastic Journey* (ed. Patrick Hart), Kansas 1977, 87ff.

9. See Y. Congar, *A History of Theology*, New York 1968, 171–4.

10. See B. Collett, *Italian Benedictine Scholars and the Reformation*, Oxford 1985, chs. 4–8; also 'The Benedictine Origins of a Mid-Sixteenth-Century Heresy', *The Journal of Religious History* (Sydney) 14/1, June 1986, 17–18.

11. Jean Leclerq, *The Love of Learning and the Desire for God*, New York 1961, 189–231.

12. *The Constitution of the Society of Jesus* (ed. and trans. George E. Ganss), St Louis, Missouri 1970, no. 351, 446, 464.

13. E.g., the former Jesuit General John Roothaan's treatise *De Ratione Meditandi*. See J. Roothaan, *Exercitia Spiritualia S. P. Ignatii de Loyola. Versio Literalis ex autographo Hispanico notis illustrata*, Ratisbonae 1923, Appendix II, 460–528.

14. See John C. Meagher, 'And the Word became Spirit', *Continuum* 1/3, 1991, 4–29.

15. For a more precise formulation of this observation, see A. Pieris, 'Woman and Religion in Asia: Towards Buddhist and Christian Appropriation of the Feminist Critique', *Dialogue*, New Series, Vols. xix–xx, 1992–1993, 181–6. See also Langdon Gilkey's remarks appropriated and commented upon in A. Pieris, *Love Meets Wisdom* (n. 2), 10, 28, 113.

16. Cf. Helmut Peukert, *Science, Action and Fundamental Theology. Toward a Theology of Communicative Action*, Cambridge, Mass. 1984, 143–245.

17. A. Pieris, 'Does Christ Have A Place in Asia?', *Concilium* 1993/2, 37–42.

III · Theological Method

Exegesis and Systematic Theology – The Exegete's Perspective

Klaus Berger

The relationship between exegesis and systematic theology has not always been problematical, but only since the rise of the historical-critical method. Until then, any scriptural exegesis was the argumentative part of a systematic-dogmatic position. It was in the Enlightenment that the historical-critical method first gained its independence and became an independent theology with an independent, implicit dogmatics and ethics. One can find an account of this in various studies on hermeneutics. Under the heading 'Hermeneutics' one often finds a hidden systematic theology of the exegete concerned. In my view this state of affairs is totally undesirable. First of all, it is the basis for a disastrous entanglement of scriptural exegesis and systematic theology among both exegetes and systematic theologians; and secondly, it makes dialogue between exegetes and systematic theologians difficult, because whereas both should really, first and foremost, be talking about their particular systematic theologies, exegetes as a rule do so as if they were interpreting 'scripture in itself'. One good example of this is the most recent discussion about the texts on the resurrection in Germany sparked off by Gerd Lüdemann's book *The Resurrection of Jesus* (1994): in it the controversial exegete has put forward an anti-supernaturalism with systematic elements from 'liberal' theology.

One interesting special case of the misuse depicted above is the imperceptible adoption of positions from Protestant systematic theology in the exegesis of 'progressive' Catholics: thinking that exegesis is free of systematic theology, well-meaning critics of the church have often adopted massive Protestant systematic theology or even philosophy without noticing what they were taking on and what they had attached themselves to. One example is the assessment of 'works' in Catholic exegesis of Paul or hostile criticism of mysticism. As a rule Catholic modernism is associated with massive uncritical rationalism. Where the modern human sciences are taken as a guideline, unchangeable anthropological constants are usually presupposed; these may even become a new systematic theology, as could be demonstrated from the dogmatic function of theses from e.g. Freud or Jung in modern psychological exegesis.

From this we may conclude that the relationship between exegesis and systematic theology often involves a dispute between contemporary positions in systematic theology, the content of which is in fact different. Exegetes often instil a sense of terror in this dispute, because philological arguments usually have a stronger effect than those from systematic theology. It is particularly easy to infiltrate lightly disguised systematic positions into academic exegesis, as it is difficult to see through them.

How in the face of this there could be a healthier relationship between the two disciplines can be described in a series of theses. Here I shall make a distinction in principle between exegesis and application. By exegesis I understand a reconstruction of the view and purpose of a particular biblical author, and by application its 'relevance' for the present. My argument is that the two stages should be kept separate in terms of both method and content.

1. *Exegetes are called on to give an account of their implicit dogmatics. The aim of this process is the self-critical perception of the limits set to modern rational science by the nature of their questions and methods.*

Neither 'faith' nor any magisterium should set limits to the scientific investigation of the Bible, but exegetes would do well to concede that with their methodology they can achieve only what is capable of intersubjective perception. The methods of exegesis are also those of other cultural disciplines. And it is not the methods which make exegesis a theological discipline, but the audience to which it is addressed, namely the 'church'.

Furthermore, exegetes should give an account of their standpoint and the perspective to which that gives rise. However, that does not mean that they should be content with this standpoint.

2. *On the contrary, a real division of labour between exegesis and dogmatics is necessary. For the exegete is the advocate of the distinctive, irreplaceable role of scripture (the canon).*

In contrast to other religions (e.g. to Mithraism), Christianity has achieved a theology. Thus in principle something like a division of authorities has already been introduced into this religion in a concern for normativeness. Since the Enlightenment this has also existed within theology.

3. *A division of labour between exegesis and dogmatics is in the end and* a priori *open. Otherwise theological work as a whole would be superfluous.*

If one achieves theology at all, then this cannot just consist in preparing what is believed for teaching. What is involved is, rather, a shared struggle over what can be the truth at a particular time. For truth in the biblical sense is not an eternal doctrine, but consists primarily in achieving living fellowship with Jesus Christ.

This understanding of truth, which is distinct from a primarily doctrinal understanding, can be justified as follows. When Jesus says 'I am the truth', he does not of course mean by this a correspondence between object and judgment, but the reliability of his person. This truth is expressed in the fact that one can constantly build on Jesus, that his word is valid and his power holds. Moreover, it is not facts which can be isolated that are 'true', but particular experiences of steadfastness, etc. From a biblical perspective the 'truth' of facts and events is decided only by whether they are an expression of this steadfastness. Now if this truth is a matter of steadfastness, future evidence plays a special role. Similarly, it becomes clear that faith is not just based on individual facts but to some degree by definition is based on a coherent chain of demonstrations of God's care, on his steadfast faithfulness. This characteristic of biblical faith preserves us from a pernicious isolation of individual data in a 'take it or leave it' way.

Dogmatic truth is derived from the 'true' living relationship just described, as an attempt also to gain a theoretical grasp of this relationship of discipleship; there is then a reciprocal reaction between theory and praxis. Such a theoretical grasp of truth comes about in two ways: as a rule of life (morality) and as confession. Such a theoretical understanding and linguistic formulation is necessary because language (like signs generally) is an essential element of human society. The relationship between church and theoretical truth is to be understood as the church reflecting on that by which it lives. But because life – again by definition – is radically historical, theoretical truth will also have extremely topical elements as its content, as well as those elements which connect it with the past. I see the former more in morality and the latter more in the confession. It is helpful and in my view also honest in the case of theoretical truth to begin from a limited consensus and a limited universality. That is necessary simply to avoid giving the illusion that it is not God but dogmatics which are eternal, and that eternity in the biblical sense means immovable rigidity. Rather, eternal life means the vitality of the living God. One of the consequences – already long practised by Rome in relation to the Uniate Eastern churches – is a priority of the fellowship of love (or communion with Rome) over the strict identity of the confession.

Accordingly, in this view dogmatic theology and confession are not superfluous, but are and can be understood as a factor derived from the life of the church and thus strictly as 'church' dogmatics.

For this reason scholarly discussion cannot consist in the repetition or endorsement of statements of the magisterium. Scholarly discussion in fact needs free space, which the magisterium should calmly grant it. Conversely, academic theologians should not understand themselves as 'the' magisterium of the church.

4. *In application, scripture cannot be understood in the sense of a law which applies directly; the important thing is loyalty towards it, which the exegete has to inculcate.*

Neither the letter of scripture nor what exegetes discover as its historical meaning can apply directly, now. The reason for this is that the statements of the scripture of the Old and New Testaments are varied, differ from one another historically, and therefore cannot simply be transferred to later situations.

Rather, the questions thrown up by historicism must be taken up fearlessly for the sake of the truth. This understanding of the truth fits surprisingly well with what scripture says of itself when it calls Jesus Christ himself the truth. That means that truth does not consist primarily in an identical programme, but predominantly in the fellowship of disciples with the one who is himself the truth. It means that unity in love and a living relation with Jesus Christ have a higher degree of relevance than statements of faith.

On the other hand, what the first witnesses say about the actions and words of Jesus is of basic importance for anyone who wants to come into contact with Jesus Christ in any way at all. The canon is the only way of not making this intended fellowship with Jesus Christ an arbitrary one, but rather turning to Jesus as he understood himself. Really to take Jesus seriously in this way and not to replace him by wishful thinking is the special task of exegesis. In calling this loyalty, I am distinguishing it from arbitrariness and randomness on the one hand and from a biblicistic or purely legalistic reading of scripture on the other.

5. *From the perspective of the exegete, systematic theologians should have more courage to do real systematic theology and not regard themselves primarily as historians of dogma.*

Precisely when exegetes really exert themselves to be advocates of the witness of the first disciples, and do not do their own dogmatics on the side, it becomes important for systematic theologians really and consistently to perceive their own role. And it is quite clear that they must not just repeat what the exegete says, nor must they just describe what others have thought; rather, from what exegetes have presented to them as the wealth of scripture they must choose thoughtfully what 'urges Christ' in the present. And in no way must the application which then emerges be identical with exegesis. For it will always be necessary to enter consistently into the contemporary culture.

It would therefore be naive to require systematic theologians to work 'scripturally'. Rightly understood, they cannot do that. All that they can do is in each individual instance to listen to scripture or exegesis as long as possible and not thoughtlessly overlook or push to one side what emerges from it. But unfortunately that is not done, and an honest reckoning needs to be taken time and again of what is added. For systematic theologians must not just select from scripture on particular occasions but include in what they say imagination, specialist knowledge, knowledge of the world, what is taught by the media, church tradition and philosophy, as an expression of a particular understanding of themselves and the world. The aim of their task is not an abstract biblicism in which the exegetes could triumph; the goal can only be to give convincing form to the truth of discipleship at a particular time. For the finest systematic theology is no good if it does not move people, and its criterion is living discipleship in the strictest sense of the word.

6. *Exegetes do not regard their historical-critical approach to scripture as the only possible one, but as the only scientific one.*

There is no disputing the fact that there are many ways to scripture; in addition to exegesis, there are for example the liturgy, the graphic arts, liberation theology or meditation. That has always been the case in the church, and it will continue to be so in the future. The Bible was not written just for exegetes. And often exegetes find that they only really get into a text when they have to preach on it, and that this also helps them further in their exegesis.

However, the methods of exegesis are fruitful and irreplacable for particular instances. In disputes over the Bible, the methods of historical-critical exegesis are instruments of peace which simply prevent differences of opinion from being resolved by violence. For exegesis is concerned with arguments and proofs; the reason is addressed. Despite all experiences of the impotence of reason, despite the awareness that reason is also a 'whore', as Luther remarked, one must concede that there is a certain international consensus, a certain band of possibilities within which one can come to an agreement and from which one can venture to break out only by advancing arguments. Where there is a conflict over the Bible, exegesis is a kind of fire brigade. Here it does not replace the normal use of the Bible. Moreover, the experience of recent years confirms that there is a great need for factual information in church communities. Pious exegesis is mistrusted, but factual information takes hearers seriously in a special way and gives them something, and that is desirable.

7. *Exegetical and systematical theology are agreed that as theology they are descriptive disciplines, i.e. they do not regard themselves either as revelation or prophecy.*

Theology can only appear as a science among other sciences if it obeys some common rules. In some European countries this is expressed by the existence of theological faculties in state universities. Here the question whether theology is a scientific discipline really becomes acute. Here too I am concerned with a rather more modest self-understanding than *doctores sacrae scripturae* have sometimes put forward. For their words are by no means all that could be or must be said. To repeat this trite observation is particularly necessary in an age which calls itself ecumenical, in which there is or was a certain tendency to make the professor of exegesis the model for the minister. Ultimately this led to excessive demands on the exegetical disciplines even at the university, and led to great disappointment.

Here we would do well to make the division of authorities consistently a division of tasks. That does not exclude a personal union, but it does make the necessary distinctions easier; for the same person can do different things at different times, with very different aims, on the same basis (in this case scripture). There is a time for using scripture as a binding authority, prescribing it without safeguards and to some extent prophetically, and there is a time for interpreting scripture by historical criticism.

There is a time for giving guidance to many people in the church with a quite specific reference to the situation, and again there is a time for confronting all the church's preaching critically with scripture. That means that when and to the extent that one is engaged in scholarly activity one is not preaching, and vice versa. As a rule the two things have been confused in the history of Protestant exegesis. That led to professorial sermons in church or to a kind of exegesis which confused commitment with arguments.

Theology as a discipline should observe the principle of all disciplines, namely that it is open to intersubjective examination. Now that means that it does not talk about God but about human beings in respect of their religious behaviour. It is the figures of the Bible, prophets and visionaries, those who pray and preach, who talk about God. Theology has a more modest task: to describe, comprehend and think through this discourse and action, draw the consequences and get them established. But theology is neither prayer nor revelation.

That does not mean that as a theologian I could not and must not pray, but it does mean that I must distinguish between the lecture room and the pulpit. Usually this distinction is rejected as schizophrenic. In reality, however, these protests are only an expression of the well-known fact that church representatives as a rule cannot do either one or the other. As a rule they neither have a really scientific curiosity which wants to know at any price how things are, nor can they really believe and pray. Here a methodological separation seems to me to be the first step to a really honest improvement. To use a somewhat trite comparison: a gynaecologist can be married, diagnose women clinically, and at the same time love his wife.

In fact the capacity to venture on theology as a descriptive science amounts to having the confidence to consider and accept other views. For a description is concerned to present variety of biblical theologies as they are in their own right, initially leaving them just as they are, without immediately reflecting on their normativity.

There is much to suggest that this should really be risked. The advantages are obvious. First of all, this is truly catholic thought, in that it sees the unity in the multiplicity and allows the multiplicity. Secondly, it is an exercise in a basic element of faith, namely its calmness. Wherever we see blatant errors on the part of the church authorities, they derive from a lack of calmness. We can be calm if we allow others their otherness and are not anxious to make them uniform. Thirdly, one cannot be ecumenical if one is not ecumenical in one's own body; i.e., it is necessary to regard the form of one's own tradition as one among others which has only the same rights as these. Exegesis provides admirable practice in such thought.

Perhaps one thing is difficult: to have a religious conviction, a conviction on which one's whole existence is staked because it is a matter of life and death, surrender and ultimate trust – and at the same time not regard this conviction as absolute, but set it alongside others. When the church compiled the New Testament without producing a harmony of the Gospels, it possessed this wisdom. It in fact left different approaches to Jesus Christ side by side. And from the beginning the same thing was also expected of Christians in respect of Israel: this people was to be allowed to exist as God's first love. The history of Christian intolerance simply shows how much this is to ask. The reality of exegetical theologies shows that this task is not even beginning to be coped with.

8. *In questions of application, theological science cannot offer any positive legitimation, but at most introduces a veto.*

The application of scripture is primarily a matter of courage and understanding, of imagination – and not primarily of correct exegesis. Here, too, exegetes are once again a fire brigade. It is only when something is impossible that they may and must say that there is a literal misuse of scripture. Such exegesis might be the use of scripture to support racism and injustice, a violation of the first commandment or a glorification of killing. Otherwise exegetes must constantly set a biblical radicalism against the compromises that are continually made, and at every turn ask afresh whether all the possibilities have really been exhausted, for example in the direction of justice.

9. *Exegesis is fruitful to the degree that initially exegetes leave aside their own form of faith as it has developed in history and can listen to others, the biblical authors. As a second stage they must make an effort to engage both forms of conviction in critical dialogue.*

The dialogue between exegesis and systematic theology cannot succeed unless exegetes also use systematic theology as an intermediary and vice versa. So two steps are necessary for exegetes: towards detachment from their own faith and then back to faith. Neither takes place as it were privately; such steps are representative, on behalf of others in the same situation.

The question often arises whether it is at all possible to distance oneself from one's faith. The history of exegesis shows that this is a risky process which affects the whole person. One does not get very far simply with methodological doubt. But it is evident here that darkness, uncertainty and risk are of irreplaceable significance for shaping a faith which is capable of dialogue. These times are more important for the faith of the exegete than any other. Darkness, scepticism, suffering and biographical catastrophes give rise to a personal identity of faith which is no longer rigidity and parrot-like repetition but calmness in the conviction that there is a unity in and above the different forms of faith. So it is a matter of attaining the capacity to think and act in a truly ecumenical and truly catholic way. For the relationship of the individual biblical theologies to one another and to us is to be defined in a similar way to that between geographically different forms of Christianity today. In any case the question is one of unity and difference. As in an ellipse, the unity has two focal points which are in tension: God himself as the coincidence of opposites and church law as the practical use of power.

10. *Just as exegesis makes use of particular methods, so too it must give identifiable criteria for their application. From the perspective of the exegete, systematic theology is among other things also application in a scientific form.*

The history of biblical interpretation shows that scripture cannot interpret itself and that a 'canon within the canon' cannot be justified purely by exegesis. In addition, certain meta-criteria are needed which are not to be attached arbitrarily to particular contents. In my view, such criteria must be gained through phenomenology and history, starting from the fact that Judaism and Christianity are religions which take the form of the people of God. In other words, the only possible criteria are those which have both a religious and a social (ecclesiological) orientation. First to be mentioned here should be the Pauline meta-criterion of *oikodome*. One could also mention other criteria, without wanting to name them all, even if that were possible, which are at the same time both religious and ethical, like radicalism, holiness, reverence and joy. Another prime criterion must be that in the people of God no one 'falls under the table'. This simple criterion is relevant at several levels of the present discussion. It implies, for example, that neither Israel, whether Christian or not, nor any biblical author is to be excluded from the uninterrupted conversation represented by the church. It implies that the church has both a horizontal and a vertical catholicity. The exegete has the special task of functioning as an advocate of those who can no longer reply. Exegetes must perceive their functions on the one hand unselfishly (in a concern really to listen), but on the other for the benefit of those who live around them. Thus by listening closely to the ancient witnesses they provide an unavoidably necessary part of the life of the church itself: remembering. I think that criteria of this kind should take the place of formal correspondence with some statements from the past.

It should be emphasized that these criteria are not those of exegesis, but of application. They are meant as instruments for the critical investigation of proposals for using passages from the Bible. From the perspective of the exegete, in detailed exegesis, systematic theology is hermeneutical discussion about and with such criteria. But of course systematic theology is not only this but above all, and in addition to mere application, the description and development of what characterizes discipleship in relation to the present situation. Systematic theology should therefore be less an account of the general state of doctrinal opinions, and more characterized by a bold grasp of a limited situation, in full awareness of the limitations of its answer. It should above all be able to develop an encouraging vision. I think of the exegete as an honest advocate and the systematic theologian as the poet of concrete utopias. Despite their different methods, a personal union of the two is not only possible but also necessary.

The experience of church history shows that in the end the decisive thing was not theoretical games about the relationship between exegesis and systematic theology but the actual power factors, usually the tension between centralism and regional interests (including the interests of specialist disciplines). I have attempted to take account of this by starting from the priority of living church community over all theory. Community has something to do with the use of power, and here a warning must be given against any illusion. Since the days of the Bible, the church has existed as a power struggle over unity. The Bible teaches such realism, since it constantly speaks of power and its special explosiveness in relation to God. The two poles of the ellipse – the *coincidentia oppositorum* in God and church unity on the basis of church law – lie as far apart as one can imagine, but it is only together and in common that they form the mystery of the church which is always no better and no worse, no more trivial and no more high-minded, than our reality.

Translated by John Bowden

Must There be Tension Between Exegesis and Dogmatic Theology?

José J. Alemany

The approach I was asked to adopt in this article is based on the assumption that there are inevitably problems in the relationship between exegesis and dogmatic theology. This suspicion seems to suggest a tension that is damaging to theological work and which should therefore be eliminated to protect theology. Well, a tension can be eliminated in one of two ways. We can reduce to insignificance the identity and thus the effectiveness and competitiveness of one of the presumed rivals, or we can try to find a way of reconciling their respective claims that preserves as far as possible the distinctiveness and essence of each. The first alternative, theoretically easier, is obviously unjust to the silenced opponent; the second may fall into the pitfalls of a hasty eirenicism producing a superficial, if soothing, reconciliation.

However, before examining the consequences this may have for work in theology, we must take a moment to examine, from the point of view of dogmatic theology, how far and to what extent there can be said to be problems in the relationship between its work and that of exegesis.

A changed setting

Almost thirty years ago, L. Scheffczyk embarked on a defence of dogmatic theology against the danger, which he detected and denounced in certain theological circles of the time, that exegesis and the systematic transposition of its results into modern language might be considered 'the only two legitimate theological disciplines, which, as a result, would displace dogmatics in the traditional sense as superfluous'.[1] His warning was certainly justified, and it is quite easy to outline the circumstances that may have favoured such a situation. It is important to be aware of them because their influence, far from having faded, remains strong in our own day.

The main and most influential of these circumstances was probably the spectacular development achieved by exegesis and biblical studies within Catholicism in the first half of the twentieth century. It is true that this advance was not linear or uniform, or without problems, difficulties and suspicions. On the other hand, we need only see the distance between the condemnations during the shattering upheaval of the Modernist crisis (1907) and the principles established by the Constitution *Dei Verbum* of Vatican II (1965), with, in between, the moderate but effective flow of oxygen from the encyclical *Divino Afflante Spiritu* of Pius XII (1943), to note a total change of direction as regards the practice of exegesis and, in general, the involvement of science and the church with holy scripture. Through this process Catholicism, with a delay of several decades, made up the distance that had separated it from Protestant activity in this field; it was able to take over a good many methods, principles and results from Protestantism that enriched its own treatment of biblical texts.

The climate of relative freedom encouraged by these moves and the new perspectives opened up by exegetical techniques gave scripture a new and – it must be said, almost novel – attractiveness. Modern translations multiplied and sold in vast numbers. Liturgical use of the Bible in the vernacular stimulated a new interest in a better understanding, and made pastors and preachers look for a better exegetical grounding in order to present it adequately to the faithful. The church authorities issued rules intended to ensure that those required to do exegetical work as part of teaching in church institutions received a more rigorous and careful formation.

This need to take seriously, as far as possible, the new findings of biblical scholarship also made itself felt, and continues to be felt, in church movements and communities, groups of activists and study groups and courses at various levels, all of them concentrating with laudable eagerness on the text of Holy Scripture in the hope of finding there the basis of a Christian formation that they now consider essential. But what they primarily seek, perhaps, is an inspiration to sustain their lives, commitments and apostolates. It is true that this seems easier to draw from scriptural texts, whether narrative, sapiential or moralistic in character, than from dogmatic treatments that require a more intellectual approach and are therefore more distant from life. On the fringe of circles that seek a certain academic level, particularly worthy of note is the importance given to inspiration received from Holy Scripture in charismatic communities and particular trends in spirituality, but this stress has also emerged, for example, in the social analysis carried out by groups such as the Young Christian Workers.

Whereas as late as the middle of the nineteenth century the possession of a Bible was a rarity even among some church dignitaries, and Bible reading, also infrequent among this group, was the object of suspicion and even prohibition in the case of the Catholic laity, a very different situation from that obtaining, from the very beginnings of the Reformation, in Protestant circles, the development outlined above rapidly placed the Bible in the hands of all and made it a regular object of use, meditation and study.

A tense relationship?

It is no surprise that, as a result of these circumstances, which still affect our own time, and accompanying and encouraging them, exegesis should have acquired particular prominence and is forced to meet a steady demand to provide, with its special techniques, now fully integrated and recognized, resources for a better understanding of biblical texts. Nor is it surprising that I too should give it full support to carry out its task. For my part, I think that the facts I have just summarized explain the new exegetical self-confidence on the theological scene. They may not provide the whole explanation, but it is more adequate and in accordance with the facts than references to methodological or even ideological issues.

Is there any reason to see in this development a possible threat to dogmatics, reinforced perhaps by the danger referred to by Scheffczyk of its absorption by exegesis? Or does it justify us in detecting a rivalry, a 'problematic relationship', between these two areas of theology? A few other details may add their weight to this suspicion. I mention them without wishing to give them more than the status of a hypothesis, or to imply that such phenomena are widespread.

Mutual expectations of dogmaticians and exegetes

Before engaging in its task, dogmatics will have travelled (or been forced to travel) through the risky frontier area of fundamental theology. Furthermore, if it is sufficiently sensitive, it may feel it appropriate or even essential to make the criteria and questions proper to fundamental theology a permanent basis and implicit attitude of all its dogmatic theorizing. I do not believe it is necessary to list all the repercussions which the adoption of such an approach would have for theological work; I shall limit myself to mentioning the consequences arising from the incorporation of an openness to dialogue, a willingness to be exposed to various rationalities employed to justify the Christian faith in order adequately to 'give an account of the hope' (I Peter 3. 15), attentiveness to ecumenical concerns, the adoption of hermeneutical precautions, the consideration of the implications of all sorts resulting from the use of theological language and its peculiarities.

Exegesis does not include fundamental theology in its journey, nor is there any reason why it should. It uses its own methods and resources in carrying out its specific task. However, it is very likely that the dogmatic theologian will experience a certain suspicion on being presented with biblical texts that have been situated, interpreted, commented on, passed through the sieve of form criticism and redaction criticism, checked to determine their literary form, subjected to ideological and philological scrutiny, but which are in the last resort more or less defenceless in the face of any possibility of fundamentalist or literalist exploitation, or one that does not understand the questions raised by post-Enlightenment rationality (which, for the dogmatic theologian, are central).

In their turn, exegetes may feel uncomfortable at the extent to which the attitudes laboriously acquired in the application of their exegetical discipline are not always adopted by dogmatic theology, or not with the desired speed, or not in the way exegesis would feel appropriate. This could be due either to insufficient attention on the part of dogmatics to the achievements of exegesis or to the conviction that these achievements require some time before they offer a solid basis for doing theology: the time between formulation, perhaps by an individual, as a hypothesis, and when they reach the level of findings backed by a sufficient consensus of specialists. And dogmatic theologians do not always have criteria of their own by which to judge when this moment has arrived. While they think that some new exegetical attitudes have not yet become established, it is understandable that they should hold to the generally accepted data with which they are familiar, even if they are outdated.[2]

However, while there is no need to apologize for an understandable lack of technical information sufficient to keep up with the complex advances of exegetical scholarship, there is no doubt that there are grounds for dogmatic theologians to be self-critical with regard to their use of Holy Scripture in carrying out their work. In this examination of conscience they could certainly be accompanied by pastoral specialists, preachers and most church spokespersons.

More care in this area would help to avoid the use (and very often the multiplication) of quotations implying dizzying leaps through books, periods, literary forms, lack of attention to the context of a text, phrases crudely torn from their setting or used simply on the basis of a verbal coincidence with the new context into which they are being inserted. Appeals to the inspired character of scripture and all its parts is certainly not enough to justify cheerful disregard of such aspects which, of course, is not the result of ill will, but nevertheless indicates carelessness, routine or haste in the carrying out of work. In these respects, it would have to be admitted that dogmatic theologians – and not just they, though the increase in the number of 'suspects' is no consolation – have given, and continue to give, exegetes grounds for complaint.

The quest for truth

The interaction of some of the mutual expectations mentioned so far, their fulfilment of frustration (never of course total, but always to a greater or lesser degree), may have generated, or alternatively dispelled, the difficulty of the relationship between dogmatic theologians and exegetes. Nevertheless there is a perhaps more crucial sphere in which competition or collaboration between these specialists plays a role, which in addition brings us closer to the division of labour in theology. This is the quest for truth in each specialism.

Reinforcing an already growing conviction in philosophy and theology, recent investigations have again highlighted the markedly polysemic character of the term 'truth'. Doubts or reservations about the adequacy of its classical understanding (concidence between words and their object) have led to numerous attempts at reinterpretation by philosophers and theologians, directed at the understanding of truth in a wide range of contexts. These frames of reference to delimit the meaning and range of truth may be quite remote from each other, as with analyses carried out in terms of philosophy of science and discussions about the possibility of progress in inter-religious dialogue.

The result has not been that the concept of truth 'has disappeared, but that it has become a label for a wide and completely heteroclitic range of questions'.[3] While it is impossible, even if one wished, to go into all of these here, the premises on which they are based, and the implications of various sorts which they raise, perhaps we might suggest that in the task of dogmatic theologians and exegetes we find two non-coinciding forms of instantiation of the truth.

Dogmatic theologians understand their role as one of service to the 'truths of faith'. This means listening to revelation, being attentive to its development through history, its encounters with the questions posed by reason, its articulation in different human languages, the actions of the church's magisterium with regard to it. Dogmatic theology gives pointers, ultimately intended to contribute to the enlightenment that all this should bring to the believing people. The aim of its work is to collaborate in the never finished task of enabling the (revealed) Word to continue becoming incarnate plausibly and critically in (human) words, which are its inevitable vehicle.

In proceeding in this way, dogmatics will take care that its verbalization, doubtless as kenotic as the historical incarnation of the Word (because it exposes the Word to similar hazardous consequences), shows the maximum respect both for the demands of supreme Truth and for the relative coherence of partial truths. Revealed truth will lack meaning if it is not related to the partial truths, and these cannot be steamrollered or forced (though they can be subjected to 'crisis', judgment for salvation) by the splendour proceeding from the former.

From an awareness of the delicacy of their relationship to truth, dogmatic theologians can now see exegetes as colleagues also interested in establishing truth, but truth of a different kind. Truth in this context is the goal of refined specialized techniques, analysis of texts and contexts, attention to chronology and archaeology, comparative study of cultures and religions in so far as they fall within its own field of observation. In order to detect and cultivate the truth of their material, exegetes do not in principle need to know anything about the history of dogma, decisions of the magisterium (except those which directly affect its concerns), or the questions raised by the faith of the people of God.

Naturally, if they see their dedication as part of an ecclesial mission (and what else could it be, since it is here that it acquires its meaning?), exegetes cannot and ought not to remain on the sidelines of such debates, but the premise could be that the truth which it is their main aim to consolidate is philological rather than conceptual. Exegetes are more concerned to recover the original context, meaning and intention of texts than to trace the use the faith community has made of them in the course of time, or the interpretations or theoretical developments based on them in the course of the history of dogmas.

Need for collaboration

Let us return to the question underlying this whole discussion. Do these remarks, which are certainly very incomplete and open to question, justify the claim that dogmtic theology and exegesis must be in conflict? Without entering into the discussion of whether on any particular occasion the relationship has been one of mistrust and suspicion, I think that at the level of principle there is no reason at all for this division of responsibilities to have negative consequences for work in theology.

'Dogmatic theology should be so arranged that the biblical themes are presented first.' This was the recommendation of Vatican II for priestly formation (*Optatam totius*, 16). This advice highlights three things: 1. in the Council's view the two areas are indissolubly linked (clearly, this is nothing new); 2. we are in fact dealing with *two* different forms of concern with the mysteries of the faith and quest for their basis and contents; 3. precedence in time (*primum*) falls on the side of scriptural study, classically labelled 'the soul of all theology' (ibid). However, this distinction does not prevent exegetes and other practitioners of theology from joining forces to achieve common ends, *collatis viribus*, in the words of the Vatican II Constitution on Divine Revelation, concerned with wider issues than the drafting of syllabuses (*Dei Verbum*, 23).

In this way theological work, responsibly performed in different functions, working in harmony in mutual critical collaboration, can cover the range of tasks that runs from the establishment of the 'objective' meaning of biblical texts to the interpretation of the logical nexus which unifies the words uttered by God through human history in a systematic synthesis around a central core.[4]

On this journey, which is that of the long human adventure in determining what we mean by communication from God, theological statements are the product of a patient – and intellectually rigorous – listening to the Word and of the painstaking, and necessarily faith-based, systematization of its reflections. With the vitality derived from this combination of diverse forces, theology safeguards legitimate plurality without prejudice to the unity that enables it to be the bond of communion. It enriches its inherent capacity to bear witness to the truths to which it devotes itself. It includes the questions and problems of today's men and women, striving to multiply and make effective the liberating power of the message that it bears. It teaches and nourishes the people of God with the saving plans of their Lord and how best to respond to them.

Above all, theology knows that it is on a journey, and gives God glory in the aporia between the obligation of the theologian to talk about God and the impossibility for the human being to talk about God.[5] It is always at the service of the church in its permanent tension as it strives for the fullness of divine truth (cf. *Dei Verbum* 8), a companion and inspirer in the stages, sometimes difficult, sometimes joyful, often full of uncertainty about many basic questions, which make up the nomadic life of human beings today.

Translated by Francis McDonagh

Notes

1. L. Scheffczyk, 'Dogmática', in E. Neuhäusler and E. Gössmann, ¿Qué es teología?, Salamanca, 1969, 231–58, quotation 232 (original ed. Was ist Theologie?, Munich 1966). The ideas contained in this article continue to be very valid and suggestive for our subject.
2. For other exegetical reservations about dogmatics, cf. ibid., 243ff.
3. A. Kreiner, Ende der Wahrheit? Zum Wahrheitsverständnis in Philosophie und Theologie, Freiburg 1992, 3 and esp. 465–74; cf. W. Beinert, Vom Finden und Verkünden der Wahrheit in der Kirche. Beiträge zur theologischen Erkenntnislehre, Freiburg 1993.
4. Cf. G. Groppo, 'Il modelo veritativo. La teologia como scienza dopo la svolta antropologica e linguistica', Salesianum 49, 1987, 728–31.
5. Cf. Karl Barth, The Word of God and the Word of Man, London 1928.

Methods in Theology: Interdisciplinary Thought in Theology

Anne Fortin-Melkevik

Introduction

Interdisciplinary work is nowadays current practice in theology. The aim of these reflections will not be to demonstrate the need for this practice but rather to provide some landmarks along the many possible ways of doing interdisciplinary work.

It is impossible to separate the way in which various interdisciplinary practices are carried on in theology from the reason for theology. Basically, the option for one interdisciplinary practice rather than another is based both on pre-established definitions of theology and fundamental choices relating to the role reserved to theology. The interaction between the discipline of theology and the other disciplines has primarily consisted in the impact on theology of concepts and categories developed in other frameworks. However, if we can say that the self-understanding of academic theology has been changed by its dialogue with other disciplines, it can equally be said that theology has transformed, then developed and reinforced, its identity as a discipline through contact with rationalities and practices of reading which have originated elsewhere. Consequently reflection on the different practices of interdisciplinary work in theology implies the question of conditions in which theology is possible within contemporary scientific paradigms.

First I shall identify one of the reasons for the involvement of contemporary theology in the problems of interdisciplinary work: openness 'to the world'. Then we shall look at four types of relationship between theology and the other disciplines, from the perspective of their influence on method in theology. After that, we shall examine the same question from the perspective of the development of a theoretical model which has inspired interdisciplinary work in theology for twenty-five years, Paul Ricoeur's model of the hermeneutical arc. Finally, we shall see that not only has the self-understanding of theology changed under the pressure of different interdisciplinary practices, but the new models also allow theology to redefine its nature and its function in society, the church and the university.

I One of the causes of interdisciplinary work: openness to 'the world'

One of the causes of the generalized practice of interdisciplinary work in contemporary theology is the introduction of new objects on which reflection is called for. The interest, following Vatican II, in experience, praxis, pluralism and, a little later, in language, text, story, has broadened the field of objects available to theological analysis. In response to these new objects, theologies of experience, of practice, of story, and so on have been developed. These theologies first of all applied theological methods to the spheres of objects hitherto external to theology. Progressively, these theologies have attached themselves to the social sciences, the human sciences and linguistics to provide themselves with adequate instruments for apprehending these 'new realities'. However, the problems are clearly reversed when objects, these new fields of theological interest, have proved to be conditions of the very possibility of the emergence of theological discourse. For example, the field of experience, at first occupied as a new field alongside the traditional fields of theological reflection, was a new chapter in theological reflection, then allowed the massive introduction of the social and human sciences into theology, and finally came to be considered a primordial condition for the legitimacy of the enunciation of any theology. The same turnaround has been made possible with the paradigm of language: linguistics first of all interested theologians in the 1960s as a new object to take into account. Then it was adopted as a methodological approach which could renew theological discourse. Today, language itself is conceived of as the proper dimension of the theological act. The profound transformations brought by the epistemological radicalization of the concepts of experience and language in theology allow us today to define the very conditions in which the theological act is possible in terms of conditions of enunciation, as linguistic acts.

Theological rationale

Theology has been led to go beyond the juxtaposition of instruments alien to its own approaches, to its own theological rationale, to accept epistemological examination of its own discourse, which has proved to be inhabited by 'other' logics. Interdisciplinary work, conceived of first in terms of adjustments and openness, has proved to be a real Trojan horse. The introduction of the instruments of these sciences has led to the consideration of new rationalities and has exploded the very definition of theology. Theology 'arising out of experience', theology as story, theology as orthopraxis, are all ways of practising theology outside the canons of *the* method of the manuals.

Thus if initially it was the opening up of the object of 'practice' which led to a move towards the social and human sciences, their adoption has made 'practices' not only the privileged object of theological research but, even more, its new foundation. The rationalities at work in these sciences no longer allow the reduction of practices (in the plural) to practice (in the singular). And once the whole field of theology has been analysed in terms of plural and polymorph practices, the return to a deductive construction of theological thought has been closed off. On the one hand, theology has been led to understand itself as social practices, practices of discourse, practices of liberation; was there still such a thing as theology (in the singular) at the end of these multiple practices? On the other hand, the adoption of linguistics has made it possible to grasp the inescapable character of the mediation of language. The introduction of the hermeneutical paradigm has turned the very conditions of the possibility of the object of theology upside down: this object can no longer be 'God'; it must rather be 'talk about God'. This discourse is no longer just the object, but the very act of theology.

The rationale of theology has been transformed. This rationale is seen to be informed by the rationalities of theologies of experience, of praxis, of language, no longer added one to another, but rather as conditions for the structuring and the emergence of the theological act itself. Interdisciplinary work, openness to the world, to other methods and other rationalities, should have allowed theology to be open to itself and to take account of its functioning and its presuppositions. However, the different practices of interdisciplinary work call for differentiated modes of articulation in connection with them, as we shall now see.

II The shock of encounter

Theology has taken different routes in its exploration of interdisciplinary work since the turning point of the last council. These different practices in interdisciplinary work have been called for by the underlying theoretical frameworks which relate to the epistemological understanding of the very meaning of the theological enterprise. The pattern of interdisciplinary work relates to the reason for theology, its definition, its role, its nature and the conditions under which it is possible, seen in connection with its confrontation with contemporary knowledge. In order to discover and classify the different practices of interdisciplinary work, I propose to present an ideal reconstruction of these implicit epistemic fields. The concepts of subject and meaning will serve to indicate different horizons which make possible the practices of interdisciplinary work.

(a) A first practice of interdisciplinary work has often consisted in importing into theology concepts and categories forged in other disciplines. These concepts and categories have then been cut off from the theoretical frameworks which explained the conditions under which they were used. In that case, interdisciplinary work was limited to the adoption of a vocabulary. Theological rationale controlled the discourse without having put itself in question. The different methodological approaches were used to discover the meaning which theology posited *a priori*. This univocal meaning was defined as being anterior to experience, to the text and practices of reading: it was to be reconstituted beyond experience, despite the text, beyond the text. The contribution of the social and human sciences in this context has been in the expression of this meaning. Contemporary categories and schemes have restated in more accessible words the eternal truths over which theology retained its power. Here the reason for theology lies in the framework of a philosophy which is both scholatic and 'modern', which produces a subject of knowledge at the service of the objectivity of the truth.

(b) In this context, the new possibilities offered by the social and human sciences have not been immediately received. The empirical subject established with full rights in these sciences, and which proceeded by an inductive approach developing the meaning rather than presupposing it, could not but explode the metaphysical framework of theology. Once accepted, the epistemological framework of the social and human sciences has in effect often led to the radical abandonment of theological rationale. Interdisciplinary work has consisted in turning theologians into sociologists, historians, who while certainly retaining a personal interest in theological questions, no longer find that their work consists in reflection based on the specific nature of the theological act. At the height of the wave of interdisciplinary work, theological rationale was considered a vestige of the past, irrelevant to contemporary discourse and rationalities. To ask 'Why theology?' in such a context has led to the disqualification of theology as knowledge relevant to expressing meaning. By internalizing the scientific ideal of objectivity characteristic of the social and human science, to the point of making it a theological ideal, theology has only indicated the relevance of its role in connection with the sphere of inter-university validation.

However, the dialogue with the social and human sciences has also led to basic practices of reflection on the nature of theology. The legitimacy of theology in the modern world could no longer be deduced *a priori* in terms of a meaning and a truth possessed from all eternity, a truth of the order of evidence. That being so, legitimacy is understood as needing to be constructed in an interdisciplinary dialogue before giving an account of its epistemological transformations to its believing subjects, the community. If theology had once been able to think of interdisciplinary work as the submission of other disciplines to its own structuring of meaning, as a juxtaposition of procedures subject to a predetermined direction, its assiduous use of the social and human sciences has now led it to understand that its meaning, its truth, can no longer remain in a special preserve. Theology has understood itself positively as one discipline among others, and as having to absorb the shock of metaphysical presuppositions which establish the conditions for the possibility of knowledge. Its nature and role have been modified internally, having been confronted with a new public space which comprises the university, society and the believing community.

(c) The introduction of a hermeneutial paradigm deriving from linguistics was no less important for theology. Under the influence of Rudolf Bultmann, the subject became the interpreting subject whose question plays a determinative role in the disclosure of meaning. This meaning, while escaping the deductive model of a certain theology, all the same escapes the control of modes of validation external to the theological rationale, since it is given in being – a being that theologians allow themselves to determine theologically. The concept of the identity of the subject-theologian who develops a theological act by appropriating his history and accepting the events of his life as they relate to the horizons of meaning in the theological texts has allowed theology to define its rationale and its role in interpretative terms. The epistemological ideal of theology has become the interpretative ideal which has allowed it to take up elements of the theological tradition. There was more scope for reflecting on the specific character of the theological act in this logic of the disclosure of meaning and the question of the interpreting subject than there was in the paradigm of the social and human sciences. This specific character had to be found at the heart of religious experience, which cannot be reduced to hermeneutical experience; since this search, the relevance and legitimacy of the interpretative theological act have been established in the community of the faith which shares the desire for a believing self-understanding of existence.

(*d*) Parallel to this openness to the social sciences, the human sciences and linguistics, the more specialized interest of structural analysis in theology has allowed a new understanding of the interpretative aim of the theological project.[1] If structural analysis was first practised in an exclusive way, it has progressively become open to a horizon which embraces semantic, rhetorical, semiotic and pragmatic approaches. These different disciplines, emerging from a common paradigm, have made it possible to put the emphasis on the work of reading as the first mode of theology. The very precise framework of the reading of the text has exploded the pretension of a privileged access to a pre-given meaning on the part of theology, to a meaning which it is the proper task of theological reason to make accessible. Theology, displaced from its supposedly privileged access to meaning and truth, has by the same token let the determination of meaning escape it. It is at this breaking point that the role of the believing subject intervenes: the reading turned towards the meaning of the text allows the involvement of the reader as a believing subject. The interface between hermeneutics and semiotics which makes possible the priority of the practice of reading represents a deepening and a ripening of the practice of interdisciplinary work in theology. After almost thirty years of different practices, the identity of theological rationale can emerge strengthened by various interdisciplinary practices of reading which, by exploding it within, open up new horizons to it.

Thus interdisciplinary work does not simply consist in openness to other disciplines, but equally in the adoption of epistemological definitions of the subject and of meaning. From the juxtaposition of different approaches, through concordism, by way of conflict and dialogue, the interpretative key of interdisciplinary work consists in identifying the metaphysical horizon against which it is articulated. It is not enough to encourage interdisciplinary work; today it is also necessary to reflect on the conditions under which the theological act is possible. Now we shall be exploring the following question: what makes possible the exercise of theological rationale today?

III The theoretical model of the hermeneutical arc as the condition under which interdisciplinary work in theology is possible

Paul Ricoeur has without doubt been one of the most striking theorists for the practice of interdisciplinary work in theology. In his writings dating from the 1970s, he develops a theoretical model which makes it possible to decompartmentalize hermeneutics and linguistics in a more scientific way.[2] His concern that both should be put on the same 'hermeneutical arc' of explication and comprehension has made possible a theoretical foundation for the complementarity of the constitution of the self and the constitution of meaning (the meaning of the text): 'the understanding of the self passes through the texts, through signs.' Paul Ricoeur posits three elements in his hermeneutical arc: 1. pre-understanding; 2. explication, which is the moment when the different disciplines of the social sciences, the human sciences and the linguistic sciences intervene; 3. the final comprehension mediated through these sciences. Interdisciplinary work is made possible, on the one hand between the different disciplines which contribute towards supporting the explication, and on the other between the moment of explication and that of comprehension. This model has been taken up many times in theology on both sides of the Atlantic, in both the English- and the French-speaking world.[3]

The possibility of interaction between hermeneutical comprehension and explanation was given a foundation in a theory of knowledge inspired by Schleiermacher, Dilthey and Gadamer. This interaction was to be formalized in the aphorism: to explain is to understand better. By contrast, the nature of the interaction between the different explicatory elements has not been given the same theoretical support, and the organizing principle of the explicatory elements has most often been the juxtaposition of disciplines serving to allow the hermeneutical goal. Ricoeur has provided foundations for interaction between explication and comprehension, but does not really enter into the conflict of epistemologies between the explicatory sciences.

The resolutions of these conflicts will arise out of the heart of the actual practices of reading. The ideal model shaped by Ricoeur has made it possible to establish passageways between the paradigms of historical-critical exegesis, biblical theology and synchronic exegesis, or between historical theology and the social and human sciences. Among other things, it also makes it possible to take up the meaning of studies in liturgy and pastoral work by means of the articulation of semiotics and pragmatics.[4] Thus the study of liturgical discourse as written discourse and discourse in action contributes complementary approaches of reading within the semiotic paradigm. The meaning of the text is no longer perceived as accessible to the naked eye, since the signification must be constructed by the reader, who is not the passive recipient of a meaning which is already present. Thus the semiotic practice of texts, biblical or others, goes by 'a practice of interpretation which involves the reader as subject'; this reading 'has its place at the very point where biblical scripture and theology are articulated, at the point which was that of the *lectio divina*, and at which from the seventeenth century there has been an epistemological break, a separation between the biblical texts subjected to critical study rather than reading on the one hand, and a theology left to ecclesial and dogmatic regulations on the other'.[5] The transition from structural analysis to semiotics has thus allowed the narrative dimension, the discursive dimension and the enunciatory dimension of the text to be taken into account; these can be open to the interpretative horizon which gives the '*subjective reference* as an orientation for theological work' and makes it possible to 'propose to the theological project an *interpretative aim* in the direction of the human subject'.[6] We are a long way from the slogan of the 'death of the subject' in these practices of reading inspired by semiotics, ranging from 'reader-response criticism'[7] through pragmatics, rhetoric and so on; a theory of the subject is being developed outside the frameworks of metaphysics, through parameters unprecedented for theology.

Narrative identity and argumentative identity

This model of the hermeneutical arc, which has been elaborated during its development, allows us to see once again the opposition between narrative readings and explicative readings which are increasingly thought of in contradictory terms in theology.[8] This opposition is central to the definition of the reason for theology, in that it is based on the very meaning of theological work: must theology interpret the foundational texts with the aid of instruments provided by the human sciences and linguistics (the hermeneutical perspective), or must it be content to describe the content of these texts, leaving aside any interference of an extra-theological kind in grasping the meaning of the text (the Anglo-American narratological perspective)? The very concept of the identity of the reader is at stake in the act of reading. In effect, the question raised is that of knowing whether the subject is constructed outside any diachronic and explicative mediation, on a narrative basis, or outside the affect, on an argumentative basis.[9] Narrative identity and argumentative identity are understood as mutually exclusive, by reason of incompatible metaphysical and epistemological horizons. The hermeneutic arc would allow these hostile perspectives to join forces without denying their own epistemic foundations.

First of all, the hermeneutical perspective makes it possible to situate narrative discourse within the process of reciprocal understanding between locutors. The narration has a place as the first element of the arc, the starting point. However, the perspective of the pragmatics of enunciation would make it possible to differentiate four elements in the interpretative process at the heart of the hermeneutical arc. Bringing out the process of reciprocal understanding shows that language is an act, and that the significance of linguistic acts is intrinsically bound up with their enunciation.

Thus there is first the element of narrative discourse, which could be the object of a pragmatic analysis, in order to disengage the form of narrative statements conceived as linguistic acts. It is at this stage that the instruments of what is currently called 'reader-response criticism' could equally make a contribution.

Secondly, however, narrative discourse moves to the interpretative register as it unfolds. This leads the locutor to justify and explain interpretations given during the narrative. Thus, thirdly, narrative discourse implies the dimension of argumentative discourse; narrative discourse implicitly becomes a discussion aimed at agreement, rather than presupposing it. This critical understanding of the agreement which is being constructed and which is envisaged at the end of a discussion has very precise metaphysical repercussions: the understanding which plays the role of an idea of reason here is not given in the being, but lies in the public space which has to be constructed. At the heart of this understanding, revision and evaluation take place through introspection, through co-operative reflection on oneself.

The fourth and final stage of comprehension consists of this reflective return over the three prior stages of the hermeneutical arc. What Ricoeur understands by the comprehension-appropriation of every process of intercomprehension derives from a synthetic and integrative reconstruction of the reasons on which the argument is based.

The stages reconstituted with the help of hermeneutics and the pragmatics of enunciation constitute the rationality of the narrative itself. Thus the narrative element is apprehended as a linguistic act aimed at mutual understanding. This approach makes it possible to show that the construction of the identity of the speaker takes place under both a narrative and an argumentative mode. So discursive explanation and analytical explanation are not opposed to narration; rather, the explicative process is included in the narration. Thus the theory of the hermeneutical arc makes it possible to re-evaluate the interaction between the spheres of aesthetical-narrative and argumentative-practical cognitive rationality which are spontaneously opposed. In this way a new space is opened for thinking out the rationale of theology by grasping the interaction between three fields of rationality, by means of the hermeneutical arc.

The attention paid to the narrative element of an aesthetic order which makes the theological act an expressive act of enunciation allows us to see that the conditions for the possibility of the theological act within the narrative framework are understood as conditions of enunciation which take on meaning in a narrative trajectory. So this resumption of the hermeneutical arc opens up new possibilities for a link between the narrative element and the practical and theoretical elements, and for giving depth to hermeneutical interpretation by means of linguistics. The concept of community becomes the normative pivot for the evaluation of the theological act, conceived of as an act of enunciation which derives from the construction of the narrative identity of the Christian as believing subject; here the community becomes the authority which allows the reading and enunciation of a believing work, the authority which validates theoretical, practical and aesthetic rationalities that take shape in linguistic acts with effects and repercussions in the lives of believers.

Conclusion

The different practices of interdisciplinary work make it possible to rethink the legitimacy and public relevance of theology. The rationale of theology finds itself first transformed and then consolidated, in and through the way in which it is exploded. In fact it has never been engaged in so many theological reflections, diverse and plural, all seeking to respond to specific questions – spiritual, cultural, political and social. Interdisciplinary work is not an end in itself, but the way taken today by theological rationale to respond to its internal demands and to external contexts.

Analysis of the discursive processes at work in the construction of religious meaning among subjects who tell and transmit their story of salvation displaces the meaning of theological work: it is no longer a matter of taking up a meaning which is delivered by one method or another, with interdisciplinary work remaining external to the logic of work on meaning. Rather, the different interactions between interdisciplinary approaches made possible by Paul Ricoeur's model allow theology to define its role in the church differently by revaluing its pastoral and spiritual functions and its function as *lectio divina*. Its role in the university is tested by the effectiveness of its practice of dialogue with the sciences; in society by the search for conditions in which it is possible to construct a narrative and aesthetic subject who is linked to the construction of an argumentative, theoretical and practical subject; in the church by the intrinsic link with subjects who enunciate their faith through their reading of the word of Another/another. In that case theology is no longer a discourse relating to a practice external to itself, or a second discourse in relation to a believing practice, according to the logic of the division between comprehension and explication. Theology is theological act as an act of enunciation which through and through constitutes the narrative and argumentative construction of Christian identity. Subject-readers in search of meaning who enunciate their faith can recognize that their identity as Christians is bound up with recognition by others.

Translated by John Bowden

Notes

1. L. Panier, *La naissance du fils de Dieu. Sémiotique et théologie discursive. Lecture de Luc 1–2*, Cogitatio Fidei 164, Paris 1991.

2. P. Ricoeur, 'Qu'est-ce qu'un texte?' (1970), in *Du texte à l'action. Essais d'herméneutique* II, Paris 1986.

3. These restatements have been very widely disseminated, thanks to the quality of the authors who have developed them. To mention just the main ones: C. Geffré, *Le christianisme au risque de l'interprétation*. Cogitatio Fidei 120, Paris 1983; D. Tracy, *The Analogical Imagination. Christian Theology and the Culture of Pluralism*, New York and London 1981; W. G. Jeanrond, *Text and Interpretation as Categories of Theological Thinking*, Dublin and New York 1988; id., *Theological Hermeneutics: Development and Significance*, New York 1991, reissued London 1994.

4. G. Bonaccorso, *Introduzione allo studio della Liturgia*, Caro Salutis Cardo, Sussidi, 1, Padua 1990; L.-M. Chauvet, *Symbole et sacrement. Une relecture sacramentelle de l'existence chrétienne*, Cogitatio fidei 144, Paris 1990.

5. L. Panier, 'Lecture sémiotique et projet théologique. Incidence et interrogations', *Recherches de science religieuse* 78/2, 1990, 209.

6. Ibid., 220 (his italics).

7. From a wealth of literature, I would mention just R. M. Fowler, *Let the Reader Understand: Reader-Response Criticism and the Gospel of Mark*, Minneapolis 1991.

8. A. Fortin-Melkevik, 'Deux paradigmes pour penser le rapport de la théologie aux sciences humaines: herméneutique et narratologie', *Laval théologique et philosophique* 49/2, 1993, 223–31.

9. Cf. J.-M. Ferry, 'Sur la responsabilité a l'égard du passé. L'éthique de la discussion comme éthique de la rédemption', *Hermes* 10, 1991, 125–37.

Theological Learning and the Study of Theology from a Teacher's Perspective

Norbert Mette

I The rationale for the study of Catholic theology

The guidelines for the structure of theological study in the Catholic church (the world church) are the *Order for the Training of Priests*, produced by the Congregation for Catholic Education. This *Ratio fundamentalis*, worked out in connection with the Second Vatican Council, was brought into force in 1970; since 1985 there has been a new version.

The Council decree on the training of priests (*Optatam totius*) rightly gave the conferences of bishops the right and the task of decreeing their own orders for the training of priests and thus also for the study of theology (cf. no. 1). Section V of this decree is concerned with the 'Revision of Ecclesiastical Studies'. By way of introduction the following general guidelines are given: 'In the revision of ecclesiastical studies the main object to be kept in mind is a more effective coordination of philosophy and theology so that they supplement one another in revealing to the minds of the students with ever increasing clarity the Mystery of Christ, which affects the whole course of human history, exercises an unceasing influence on the Church, and operates mainly through the ministry of the priest' (no. 14). An 'introductory course' at the beginning of theological study is to familiarize pupils with this fundamental theological perspective, so that further study can build on it. This further study then embraces various philosophical and theological subjects, and some indications are given of the way in which their content is to be arranged (cf. nos. 15f.). Finally, a revision of teaching methods is also advised: these methods are to ensure that quality ('an overall training which is coherent and solid') comes before quality ('over-multiplication of subjects', see no. 17).

The above-mentioned *Ratio fundamentalis* further develops these suggestions by the Council and makes them more specific. It does not seek to deprive individual conferences of bishops of the authority to prescribe their own basic orders for the training of priests, an authority which is also endorsed in CIC (no. 242), but to make it easier for them to fulfil this task. Here its special concern is 'to preserve unity and at the same time to make a healthy multiplicity possible'.

The essential points by means of which a certain unity of theological study is to be guaranteed in the church (the world church) have been taken over from this *Ratio fundamentalis* both in the Apostolic Constitution *Sapientia christiana* (1979) and in the new CIC (cc. 248–54). If we follow *Sapientia christiana* (articles 66–74) and the regulations for implementing it issued by the Congregation for Catholic Education (articles 50–54), we find that the study of theology is divided into three cycles of study. In the first cycle, consisting of ten semesters, the two years of basic philosophical study are to be completed and the theological disciplines are to be studied (specific mention is made of biblical exegesis and theology, fundamental theology, dogmatics, moral theology and spirituality, pastoral theology, liturgy, church history and canon law). In addition there are subsidiary disciplines, like 'some branches of the human sciences'. In the second cycle of studies a specialization or a focal point must be chosen in specific disciplines; in the third cycle there is the possibility of further study (for example, producing a dissertation). In further encyclicals the Congregation for Catholic Education has been concerned with detailed questions of 'church studies', e.g. the study of philosophy (1972), liturgical formation (1979), the study of the church's social teaching (1989) and the study of the church fathers.

If we are to understand all these texts on the study of theology, we should note that they take it for granted that this study has its place in the framework of the training of priests and is directly related to that. All in all, this covers more than study: in addition to 'scientific training' (cc. 248–54), on the one hand there is 'spiritual training' (244–257) and on the other 'pastoral training' (255–8). Furthermore, priestly training does not end with the first phase but is also continued in the course of the practice of priestly ministry (cc. 276.4; 279). All in all, the goal to be aimed at is that outlined, for example, by the German bishops in their basic order for the training of priests (1988):

'The focus of priestly training is the Christian who, on the basis of his personal and spiritual maturity, his theological education and his pastoral capacity, is fitted and ready:
– to live up to God's calling and to allow himself to be accepted by the

bishop into service in ordination and mission for the church as a priest with a celibate life-style for the sake of the kingdom of God;
– to continue to develop his personal, spiritual and vocational capacities in such a way that he can perform for his fellow men and women all his life the calling of Christ which he has accepted in his priestly ordination, in the pastoral situations in which he finds himself' (no. 5).

This statement is clearly based on a specific image of the priest (cf. also the lengthy statement in the introduction to the basic order), to which the efforts at training in the different spheres (spiritual, academic, pastoral) are to be organically related and harmoniously interrelated. We shall be returning to this later.

As for theological training in the narrower sense, we may say that the Vatican II decree on the training of priests, along with the more general regulations for its implementation, has led to a not inconsiderable series of positive innovations and reforms by comparison with the curriculum which had hitherto been valid and customary; special mention should be made of:

– the possibility of a curriculum which takes due account of a particular cultural context;

– an end to the need to teach or study disciplines exclusively in Latin;

– an emphasis on Holy Scripture, 'which should be the soul, as it were, of all theology' (*Optatam totius* 16);

– the replacement of the analytical method of scholastic theology (finished thesis presented by the church's magisterium – conceptual explanation – proof from the sources of faith) with a synthetic approach in dogmatics which in each instance describes the historical development of a theological doctrine, makes a speculative study of it, and connects it with present-day human problems; in contrast to a dogmatics which works with individual dogmatic statements, the aim here is to understand the connections:[1]

– openness to ecumenical questions, to a concern with other religions and world-views and references to the humane sciences;

– a concern for a 'unity of theology', however this may be more closely defined, without failing to differentiate between individual subjects and to allow a justified pluralism;

– a concern for a pastoral orientation of all theology and the integration of part of pastoral training into scientific study;

– the incorporation of insights from teaching and different methodological forms into theological study which allow room for independent and joint work by students.

However, we should note soberly that, first, the points cited have only partially and sometimes only half-heartedly been put into practice in the study of theology and, secondly, that the existing *Ratio fundamentalis* has, if anything, proved restrictive, given the enormous new developments which have taken place in theological teaching and research (and associated fields) since the last Council. In this connection we should above all note the following points:

– In the present official texts of the church the study of theology is seen exclusively in connection with training for the priesthood and accordingly the conception of it is orientated on that. No conclusions are drawn from the fact that not only candidates for the priesthood but also lay people – including women – are studying theology, and that the number of them sometimes now far exceeds that of candidates for the priesthood, not to mention that the pastoral sphere has meanwhile become very differentiated, and in addition to priests, at least in some local churches theologically trained laity and deacons are the ones mainly involved in pastoral service. In addition, we should note the presence in some regions of groups of 'lay theologians' who are preparing to be involved in religious education (teaching in schools and/or as parish catechists, and in adult education). So far the existing structure of theological study within the framework of the training of priests has to serve as the compulsory basic order for all these training programmes. Where this cannot be followed completely, as a rule reductions are simply made in the content of subjects. A fundamental restructuring of studies, for example on the basis of changed presuppositions or with a view to the variety of later spheres of activity, is unthinkable on the basis of the existing order.

– The fact that the training of priests is the binding criterion for the shaping of theological study also has a further series of problematical consequences, beginning from the fact that – wherever possible – clergy are clearly given preference in appointments to professorial chairs (and thus the question of academic competence is secondary), and along with this increasing re-clericalization efforts are now made to separate candidates for the priesthood and laity more strictly, not only in spiritual direction and pastoral training, but also in theological study. It is hard to see how this will help these two groups to work together later in pastoral practice.

– Another striking feature is the ideal of training, put forward with extraordinary harmony, that underlies the 'basic order': spiritual, academic and pastoral training supplement one another harmoniously, just as the different disciplines can be related organically to one another. There is no insight that contradictions and conflicts could arise here. At the most in cases of doubt – which quite often appear in reality – the spiritual elements are decisive in resolving the conflict.

– On the basis of the points mentioned above, it follows almost automatically that neither new approaches (for example, feminist theology) nor new contexts for doing theology[2] can find a place in the existing order of theological study. That means that encounters with the creative beginnings of theological thought must be sought outside 'official' study (something that is not necessarily welcomed); as a rule there is no critical or constructive discussion with these approaches in the context of the 'prevailing' theology.

– The tendency within the 'prevailing' theology towards a certain complacency and conservatism rather than towards a creative development of what has been handed down and towards innovation is encouraged not least by the regulations of the magisterium which for some years have had a massive influence on the shaping of Catholic theology. What is communicated to students, at least by those teaching 'secret messages', who see themselves exposed to exaggerated demands for obedience from the church's magisterium, including the threat of unilateral sanctions, should not be underestimated. Essentially it is not surprising that particularly those young people who with inner commitment and lively interest want to be trained for pastoral activity in the (Catholic) church should increasingly be giving up the study of theology in their last years in the face of the assimilation and resignation that they find all around them; but it should make us think.

– A consequence of the developments mentioned above is that in the study of theology, what is encouraged is a receptive attitude rather than an independent and critical attempt to grapple with what is presented. The preferred form of communication is largely a description of teaching – whether in the form of the results of research or a knowledge of faith presented as a compendium.

– The orientation of individual subjects on their internal systematics also means that the overall coherence of theology which is postulated – if it is – can be constructed only at a later stage and by way of addition; students at any rate cannot see a common 'logic' which runs through all theology.

II How students regard the study of theology – the results of an enquiry in Austria

Regrettably – as far as I know – there are no recent investigations which allow us to give a general verdict on how those concerned, i.e. theological students, see the existing basis for the study of Catholic theology. But so as to give at least some idea of this, by way of example, I would like to present here some findings from a survey carried out among theological students in Austria over the past year.[3] Questions were asked of candidates for the priesthood and lay theologians, both men and women, and also Protestant theological students. In summary, the findings are as follows:

– The decisive reasons for the choice of theology as a subject to study are: interest in theological questions; a need to work with people; a need to be able to give people answers to questions about their lives; clarification of one's own faith.

– For a large number of students the thought of becoming priests plays a part (that would also apply to women, if this were a possible option), but such thoughts are now being dropped by many students because they cannot accept the current image of the priest.

– Experiences of the study of theology are ambivalent. The expansion of personal horizons, grappling with the content of theology in an academic way, and greater sensitivity to social and political involvement are factors which are welcomed. Many students cannot see clearly enough the relevance of their study to personal belief.

– There is widespread criticism of the methodology of the courses and the way in which they are taught – in contrast to the positive verdict on their content.

– Suggestions for reform called especially for the following: a freer structure of studies and more possibilities of choice; a training which is more closely related to practice; the inclusion of content which is more topical or nearer to the present.

– The majority of students indicate a close connection with the church. As to their later profession what they want above all is the possibility for the church to be experienced as a community of believers or for people to be given access to a lively practice of faith. About a third want to be involved in the charitable or social work of the church or to introduce Christian values into a secular professional world. However, given their view of the existing church, they are sceptical whether the conditions for this exist.

To oversimplify somewhat, in summary the evidence may largely be interpreted as indicating that the theological students questioned were by and large content with their study, but that the majority had greater or lesser difficulties with the framework within which it was done (especially with the concrete image of the church and with the shaping of pastoral work). The fact that almost half of the theological students questioned were afraid that one day they could be in conflict with the official church and that only twenty-nine per cent of them would decide for a church post if they had to choose between equivalent posts in the church or non-church spheres clearly points in this direction. It is probably an over-simplification to want to blame all this on a mood among theologians which is all too critical of the church or even hostile to it.

Nevertheless, the church cannot and should not evade its obligations. The defects in the order of studies indicated above are too serious and the criticisms expressed by the students and the suggestions for reform they give are too serious simply to be passed over.

III Interim reflections on the teaching of theology as a presupposition for an appropriate framework of studies

When after the Second Vatican Council discussions about the necessary reform of theological study became very heated, Karl Rahner intervened vigorously at a particular phase and warned that a meaningful reform of studies had to stem from a scientific reflection on the whole of theology: 'Such reflection must consider both the unity of the one theology and the differentiation which derives from the nature of its subject-matter, and also the "epochal" form of theology which is due today. The former is a matter of course. The latter is just as important if one reflects on the time in which we live and on the kind of theology there must be if it is to do justice to the theologian as a present-day person whose faith is under severe attack.'[4] Only after such reflection could there be a well-founded decision on the canon of disciplines underlying the study of theology and the sequence in which they should be studied. By contrast, for Rahner the 'reform' which was actually taking place consisted in the preservation of the existing range of disciplines and at most the addition of further ones.

This objection on the part of Rahner was not only justified at the time but is also largely relevant even today – indeed today in particular: basically the existing curricula consist of a list of individual disciplines – which are more or less interconnected – each with its share of hours.

If this unsatisfactory state of affairs is to be overcome, what is needed, in my view, is reflection on the way theology is taught as well as academic reflection on theology as a whole; here the two are linked. However, in all sobriety we should expect that the call for reflection on how theology is taught will meet with even more rejection than scientific theoretical reflection. For teaching methods are not as a rule regarded as a constituent element of theology and its disciplines, but rather to some degree as an 'appendix' for which religious education and catechetics have a special responsibility. For theology, what is presupposed here is either a structure developed from the logic of faith or a systematics for each individual discipline, which follows from the particular methodological character of the discipline. According to this view, this structure of theology or its individual disciplines, whether dogmatic or hermeneutical, has the priority; all didactic and methodological questions are subordinate to it.[5]

Those who argue like this are betraying complete ignorance of the issues either in reflections on teaching methods or even in the academic sphere. To think that all that is necessary is to devise and practise techniques and skills which make it possible to communicate content as efficiently as possible to those who are learning or studying is a misunderstanding. Furthermore, reflections on teaching method are not aimed at a lowering of standards or an adaptation of the content to the method – at the risk of abandoning the content. Rather, reflections on teaching method of any substance content take place on a number of levels:

(a) They consider the anthropological and socio-cultural presuppositions present in the concern to communicate certain 'objects of learning' which need to be taken into account (which can also mean changing or transforming them). (b) They determine the aims, contents, methods and media for a 'subject' and attempt to relate these more harmoniously. (c) In so doing such discussions allow themselves to be guided by the insight that the aspects of the 'subject' in question are not purely external, but play a part in shaping it – just as those on the receiving end also have an active influence on it, so that a 'subject' changes in the process of being learned. What is necessary, therefore, is to reconstruct this 'didactic logic' of the subject being taught and those who are actively learning it, along with the interactive relationship between them. This is the genuine question of a 'didactics of knowledge' which in turn is closely related to scientific theory: following Piaget, in practical terms one could describe this as 'genetic epistemology'.

Applied to theology, this means that theology cannot be understood as an objective entity the content of which can be noted and appropriated as knowledge. Rather, knowing, learning, reflecting and understanding in 'matters' of faith are already genuinely theological processes which have to correspond to the 'matter' under consideration – and vice versa. To this degree the didactic element also has a deeply theological status.[6] Here the fact that theology is not about a knowledge which can be learned (cumulatively) and then applied is taken seriously for the connection between teaching and learning. Theology involves the communication of a reality and an account of it which in turn requires to be communicated appropriately. Helmut Peukert's statement, 'What is meant determines the way in which it may possibly be communicated intersubjectively, and conversely must be inferred from the process of communication',[7] can also to some degree be read as the basic didactic formula for doing theology.

One can say that the close connection between theology and the shaping of study which arises from this was known in the academic theological tradition not only as a place of learning but also as a place for living and this was maintained – even if the accent fell on different places – until in the course of the 'academizing of theology', with its specialization and positivization, theology came to split into separate disciplines.[8] From this perspective we should assess quite positively the way in which the Roman order of study described above is concerned to maintain this connection. But as has been shown it does this in terms of an understanding of theology fixated on a certain notion of orthodoxy. It seems that to the degree that a changed theological paradigm is becoming established, and theology is being understood and practised more markedly in the sense of 'doing theology', the connection between content and learning, understanding and action, is again coming into its own in a new way. It is no coincidence that remarkable new forms of doing and learning theology have developed, say, in the context of feminist theology or liberation theology; what is characteristic of them above all is that the different dimensions of theological education – science, spirituality and praxis (in both the church and society) – interpenetrate one another strongly so as to supplement one another critically and constructively and do not lead to a general levelling down.

IV Didactic postulates for a reform of theological study

The reflections so far on an appropriate approach to teaching theology suggest that some conceptual alternatives as they have been constructed and contrasted in the discussion of the reform of studies in recent years[9] have become a problem, for example where a distinction has been made between theology as a subject to be taught and theology to be used in a profession, or between an existential and a professional or pastoral basic concept. These are not fundamental differences, but rather possible focal points or aspects which then also have consequences for other spheres. Thus for example study which is in general more markedly orientated on a field of activity at the same time increases the didactic demands on individual disciplines instead of reducing them. So the following didactic postulates attempt to consider not just one or another but the whole web of existence, scholarly knowledge and profession. Their starting point is the considerable change in the presuppositions for the study of theology: not only can it no longer be taken for granted that students have been socialized by the church, but there is a pluralism within theology itself, and the professional spheres of male and female theologians are different. Here theology should help in the attainment of a capacity for theological judgment, combined with competence in pastoral action 'which makes possible "thought and action in the spirit of Jesus" in the light of the present situation'.[10]

(a) The principle of learning by example has to take the place of cumulative learning. The reason why cumulative learning has so far been dominant in theological study is connected with the differentiation of individual disciplines which has come about and the notion that students should familiarize themselves with at least the basic knowledge in each individual discipline. This has necessarily led to an accumulation of the content of knowledge, and it is this that is finally tested in examinations. In this way students experience theology as an addition of these individual disciplines. They are largely left alone with the question how they belong together. The timetable is so full that hardly any space is left. By contrast, learning by example means getting rid of the idea that all possible content must be communicated; instead of this the students – along with the teachers – are led to grapple with a selection of complex theological questions which are to be solved by taking note of their different dimensions (e.g. biblical, historical, dogmatic, psychological, etc), and with the help of the relevant disciplines. The advantage of such a study project[11] is that it is possible to learn by means of a particular problem how the different spheres within theology belong together (here this unity need by no means always turn out to be organic, but can prove to be unwieldy) and at the same time makes possible a cooperative insight into the 'logic' of the individual disciplines. In addition, study can be more orientated on praxis without lacking in theory.[12]

(b) The principle of learning by example gives participatory learning priority over receptive learning. Participatory learning means that those who are learning or studying can play an active part in shaping the process of learning – and research. This is by no means a new idea, but underlies the classical notion of the university as a community of teaching and learning. Accordingly, teaching and learning are to be understood and conceived of in a reciprocal relationship. This is most explicit in investigative learning together. But the independence and active participation of the students can be encouraged even in the propaedeutic realm. This happens in particular not only by the communication of content but also – again by way of example – by a reconstruction and critical evaluation of the processes of knowledge. These observations by no means seek to deny that receptive learning cannot be totally dispensed with. But such learning is misguided where it is required only because of a particular type of material and does not lead to the possibilities of participatory learning.

Both must always stand in a sound relationship to each other; in connection with the present pattern of studies, that means that the number of possible choices must be considerably increased.

(c) Particularly in theology and its study, another aspect is associated with participatory learning. As the Austrian survey shows, to a considerable degree this involves a person's own belief and thus his or her whole existence. Here learning theology can sometimes be experienced as disconcerting and sometimes as liberating: quite often it leads to crises in the course of which previous faith can be transformed. That means that students are anything but a *tabula rasa* which has first of all to be filled with theological teaching. They already bring along their individual theologies. To be able to state this explicitly and work it out is not just a matter for spiritual direction. It must also be a concern of theological study in the sense of a critical-discursive reassurance – in the sense of existential learning – if it is really to set in motion a lifelong process of learning theology and not allow scientific-critical reflection and spiritual edification to drift apart in a pernicious way.[13] Theological existence includes lifelong training and maturing in both spheres – together with the resultant crises and transformations, which are both existential-psychological and intellectual-cognitive.

(d) If students are to acquire a power of theological judgment which is appropriate today, it is necessary for the study of theology to be conceived of as ecumenical learning. It is characteristic of ecumenical learning[14] that it aims at an awareness of the world church and is equally sensitive to a person's own context; that it takes into account the whole of ecumenical Christianity and makes it capable of intercultural and religious dialogue; and that it allows itself to be guided by a concern for the present and future living conditions of all human beings and a habitable earth. This cannot and need not be developed in detail here. I would merely recall that particularly in the sphere of the Catholic church a well-tried tradition can be taken up which needs only modification to be continued. If such experiences of the world church and the ecumene are also to be had in study – and this is worth devoting all our energy to – then all ways should no longer lead just to Rome but all over the world.

Translated by John Bowden

Notes

1. Cf. K. Rahner and H. Vorgrimler, *Kleines Konzilskompendium*, Freiburg 1966, 291.

2. Cf. *Concilium* 115, 1979, *Doing Theology in New Places*.

3. In what follows I shall be referring to the brief account of the enquiry by C. Friesl, published in duplicated form, *TheologiestudentInnen '93: Identität und Beruf*, Vienna 1993.

4. K. Rahner, *Zur Reform des Theologiestudiums*, Freiburg im Breisgau 1969, 21.

5. This position is expressed particularly evocatively by J. Ratzinger, *Die Krise der Katechese und ihre Überwindung*, Einsiedeln 1983, esp. 14f.

6. Cf. in more detail J. Werbick, 'Religionsdidaktik als "theologische Konkretions-wissenschaft". Zum theologischen Rang des Didaktischen – aus fundamental-theologischer Perspektive', *Katechetische Blätter* 113, 1988, 82–99.

7. H. Peukert, *Wissenschaftstheorie – Handlungstheorie – Fundamentaltheologie*, Düsseldorf 1976, 318.

8. For the historical lines of development in the study of theology cf. H. Luther, *Hochschuldidaktik der Theologie*, Hamburg 1980, 7–105.

9. Recorded e.g. in the six-volume documentation *SKT – Studium Katholische Theologie*, edited by the commission 'Curricula in Theologie' of the Westdeutscher Fakultätentag by E. Feifel, Zürich, Einsiedeln and Cologne 1973–1980.

10. W. Fürst, *Praktisch–theologische Urteilskraft*, Zurich, Einsiedeln and Cologne 1986, 220. For closer material definitions see the previous articles in this volume.

11. Cf. e.g. G. Otto, 'Curricula für das Studium der Praktischen Theologie?', in F. Klostermann and R. Zerfass (eds.), *Praktische Theologie heute*, Munich and Mainz 1974, 567–85, esp. 579ff. For a corresponding overall conception of study cf. especially D. S. Browning, *A Fundamental Practical Theology*, Minneapolis 1991.

12. For an appropriate definition see W. G. Jeanrond, 'Between Praxis and Theory: Theology in a Crisis over Orientation', *Concilium* 1992/6, 49–56.

13. In this connection we should recall Rahner's conception of a 'basic course' of theology, which is meant to progress a 'first stage of reflection' in order to move the students from where they stand and introduce them to academic theology; cf. Rahner, *Reform* (n. 4), 51–96.

14. From the considerable literature on the topic I would refer here to G. Orth (ed.), *Dem bewohnbaren Erdkreis Schalom. Beiträge zu einer Zwischenbilanz ökumenischen Lernens*, Münster nd; K. Piepel, *Lerngemeinschaft Weltkirche*, Aachen 1992.

Are human beings destroying humanity?

Most of us know the figures by heart. At the time of Christ's birth there were around 200 million people in the world. By 1800 the earth's population had reached a billion. By 1900 it had doubled to two billion, and between 1926 and 1976 it rose to four billion. The 1980s saw the five billion mark passed, thus reaching the point when there were more people than had ever lived in the whole of human history.

Today there are three more people each second, 10,000 each hour, 98 million each year. Humankind is increasing by a billion every decade.

The present world population numbers around 5.7 billion. Prognoses for the year 2050 differ, fluctuating between 7.9 billion and 12 billion. Forecasts for 2150 range between 11.6 billion and 28 billion.

When is the world overpopulated? A great variety of criteria can be used. The definition of Lester Brown, Director of the World Watch Institute, is: 'The world is overpopulated when the production of food cannot keep pace with the growth in population.' To judge from what was said at the world population conference, last year food production declined for the first time. The definition of the biologist Paul Ehrlich is: 'A country is overpopulated when it destroys its basic natural resources.' According to this definition the rich countries of the North are over-populated. The people in these rich countries, which represent twenty per cent of the population, are consuming eighty per cent of total world resources each year. The rich fifth of the world population must realize that its consumerism and modern technologies are destroying Planet Earth and its environment. If the other four-fifths of humankind were to claim the same behaviour and same technologies for themselves, the human species would be finished.

The United Nations took up this problem at a relatively early stage. The 1968 International Conference on Human Rights in Tehran proclaimed the human right to birth control. The first World Population Conference in Bucharest in 1974 put the fight against structural poverty in the foreground: 'The main foundation for an effective solution of population problems is socio-economic change.' Karan Singh, the then Indian Minister of Health, reduced this to the formula, 'Development is the best form of contraception'. The formula 'a new world economic order', which was to guarantee a just distribution of resources, was coined at that time.

In Bucharest the representatives of the poor South felt that the delegates of the rich North with their plans for reasonable birth control were engaged in a plot discriminating against the poor. I clearly remember a good Peruvian friend saying to me at that time: 'Birth control is a form of neocolonialism of you rich against us poor.'

But in the meantime, despite everything, the earth has moved somewhat. At the second World Population Conference in Mexico City in 1984 the attitude of the countries of the South changed somewhat, particularly in the face of the growing international debt crisis. The majority of governments in the southern hemisphere recognized that the abundance of children was a problem. Mwai Kibaki, the Vice President of Kenya, remarked that when it came to birth control it was no longer 'a matter of whether but of how'.

There was a consensus over accepting the two Final Documents of the Bucharest and Mexico City conferences, but the Vatican immediately distanced itself from it. It regarded both the propagation of different methods of contraception and the way in which married couples and the unmarried, above all youth, were put on the same level as an attack on morals and the family.

What are the main causes for this development of the world population which is so dangerous for humankind? Without wanting to give an exhaustive account, I would point above all to three causes which have an effect on one another.

First comes structural poverty, above all in the countries of the southern hemisphere. Structural poverty means that our actual world economic situation is shaped by structures which further intensify the divide between the rich North and the poor South. The South loses around $500 billion per year simply through the trade restrictions of the rich nations on the countries of the South.

Then there is the massive discrimination against women. So an improvement of the social, political, legal and economic status of women is of the utmost significance. An improvement in the basic education of girls and women is very important in this connection. For the highest decreases in birth rate are always achieved where women are given more rights, where they have access to education and jobs, and where health care for women is improved. Bangladesh is constantly mentioned as a good example in this respect. The number of births has fallen, though living conditions have not generally improved.

The third cause is the lack of possibilities for women in the poor countries of the south to use contraceptives. Certainly the number of couples who use contraceptives has increased from fourteen to fifty-three per cent worldwide since 1970. But more than 300 million couples have no access to safer and more effective methods of birth control.

During the course of the Third International Conference on Population and Development in Cairo and after it, a certain international consensus developed primarily over the following points:

1. There is a human right to birth control. Today this is also recognized by most representatives of the southern countries and marks progress from the first conference in Bucharest.

2. Abortion and compulsory sterilization cannot be means of birth control.

3. The overcoming of structural poverty in the world and above all a change in the consumerism of the rich North is urgently necessary.

4. The position of women must be improved in every respect; above all they must be able to receive a better basic education.

5. Special action plans for contraception to be made available comprehensively are urgently necessary.

6. Reproductive health is important. In the words of the Cairo action plan, this means 'the right to information and access to safe, affordable and practicable means of regulating fertility and the right of access to appropriate health services which enable women to have a safe pregnancy and birth and help parents to have a healthy child.' Also connected with this is sex education for young people, help for men and women to gain insight into their health problems, investigation and treatment of sexual diseases, pre- and post-natal care for mothers, and injections for babies and small children.

It is alarming that before and during the conference the religious fundamentalists, above all the Islamic fundamentalists and the Vatican, united to fight against the Cairo action plan.

To the Vatican it must be said quite emphatically: one cannot be against abortion and against 'artificial means of contraception'. There is no reasonable theological basis for repudiating 'artificial contraception' on theological or ethical grounds. In opposing reasonable birth control, the Vatican is taking a share of the responsibility for unwanted pregnancies and their consequences. With this position should be compared what the Second Vatican Council said about responsible parenthood. That means that parents themselves must decide, in responsibility for themselves, their children and the whole world, how many children they want to have.

Norbert Greinacher

The editors of the Special Column are Norbert Greinacher and Bas van Iersel. The content of the Special Column does not necessarily reflect the views of the Editorial Board of Concilium.

Contributors

JAMES M. BYRNE was born in 1960. He is the Elrington Research Fellow at the School of Hebrew, Biblical and Theological Studies, University of Dublin (Trinity College). He holds an STL in Fundamental Theology from the Gregorian University, Rome, and a PhD in Theology from the University of Dublin (Trinity College). He recently edited *The Christian Understanding of God Today* in celebration of the quatercentenary of Trinity College and has written articles in the fields of hermeneutics and theological method.

Address: 14 The Spinnaker, Castle Avenue, Clontarf, Dublin 3, Ireland.

ROGER HAIGHT is a Jesuit of the New York province. He is Professor of Historical and Systematic Theology at Weston School of Theology in Cambridge, Massachusetts. He received his doctorate in theology from the University of Chicago in 1973 and has held teaching positions in Manila, Chicago and Toronto before moving to Cambridge. He is the author of *The Experience and Language of Grace* (New York 1979), *An Alternative Vision: An Interpretation of Liberation Theology* (New York 1985), *Dynamics of Theology* (New York 1990), and many articles in the areas of fundamental theology, christology, ecclesiology, the theology of grace and spirituality. He is currently the President of the Catholic Theological Society of America.

Address: Weston School of Theology, 3 Phillips Place, Cambridge, Massachusetts 02138–3495, USA.

CARL REINHOLD BRÅKENHIELM was born in 1945. He is Professor at the Faculty of Theology in Studies in Faiths and Ideologies, Uppsala University, Sweden; he is a minister in the Lutheran Church of Sweden and also a member of the Doctrinal Commission of its General Synod. Several of his books have been published in English: *How Philosophy Shapes Theories of Religion* (1975), *Problems of Religious Experience* (1985) and *Forgiveness* (1993); so have two articles in *Studia Theologica*:

'Is Metaphysics Theologically Possible?' (1989) and 'Constructive Theology and the Study of Popular Life-Philosophies' (1990). He is also the editor of *Power and Peace. Statements on Peace and the Authority of the Churches* (Uppsala 1992).

Address: Uppsala University, Department of Theology, Box 1604, S 75146 Uppsala, Sweden.

DAVID TRACY was born in 1939 in Yonkers, New York. He is a priest of the diocese of Bridgeport, Connecticut, and a doctor of theology of the Gregorian University, Rome. He is the Greeley Distinguished Service Professor of Philosophical Theology at the Divinity School of Chicago University. He is the author of *The Achievement of Bernard Lonergan* (1970), *Blessed Rage for Order: New Pluralism in Theology* (1975), *The Analogical Imagination* (1980), and *Plurality and Ambiguity* (1987).

Address: University of Chicago, Divinity School/Swift Hall, 1025 East 58th Street, Chicago, Ill. 60637, USA.

NICHOLAS LASH was born in India in 1934. A Roman Catholic, he has been, since 1978, Norris-Hulse Professor of Divinity in the University of Cambridge. Hs publications include: *His Presence in the World* (1968); *Change in Focus* (1973); *Newman on Development* (1975); *Voices of Authority* (1976); *Theology on Dover Beach* (1979); *A Matter of Hope: A Theologian's Reflections on the Thought of Karl Marx* (1981); *Easter in Ordinary: Reflections on Human Experience and the Knowledge of God* (1988); *Believing Three Ways in One God: A Reading of the Apostles' Creed* (1992).

Address: University of Cambridge, Faculty of Divinity, The Divinity School, St John's Street, Cambridge, CB2 1TW, England.

JOHN E. THIEL is Professor of Religious Studies at Fairfield University, Fairfield, CT. He is the author of *Imagination and Authority: Theological Authorship in the Modern Tradition* (Minneapolis 1991), and *Nonfoundationalism*, Guides to Theological Inquiry (Minneapolis 1994).

Address: Fairfield University, Dept of Religious Studies, Fairfield, Connecticut 06430–7524, USA.

ALOYSIUS PIERIS, a Sri Lankan Jesuit, was born in 1934. He is the founder-director of the Tulana Research Centre in Kelaniya near Colombo. A classical Indologist who has specialized in Buddhist philosophy, he is now engaged in a vast research programme on mediaeval Pali (Buddhist) philosophical literature, on which he has begun publishing a series of papers. He edits *Dialogue*, an international review for Buddhists and Christians published by the Ecumenical Institute, Colombo. He has written extensively on missiology, theology of religions, Asian theology of liberation and Buddhology. He is the author of *An Asian Theology of Liberation* (New York 1988) and *Love Meets Wisdom* (New York 1988). He is visiting professor at the Asian Pastoral Institute, Manila and has also held the Franciscan Chair of Mission Studies at Washington Theological Union (1987), the Henry Luce Chair of World Christianity at Union Theological Seminary, New York (1988) and the Ann Potter Wilson Distinguished Chair of Theology at Vanderbilt University, Nashville (1992).

Address: Tulana Research Centre, Kohalwila Road, Gonawala, Kelaniya, Sri Lanka.

KLAUS BERGER was born in Hildesheim, Germany, in 1940. He studied philosophy, oriental studies and theology in Munich, gaining his doctorate there in 1967. From 1970 he taught at the Rijksuniversiteit in Leiden, gaining his Habilitation in Hamburg; from 1974 he has been Professor of New Testament Theology in Heidelberg. His many books include: (on the history of religions) *Die Auferstehung des Propheten*, 1977; *Die Amen-Worte Jesus*, 1972; *Die Gesetzesauslegung Jesu*, 1972; *Das Jubiläenbuch*, 1981; *Qumran und Jesus*, ⁵1993; *Manna, Mehl und Sauerteig*, 1993; (on methodology) *Formgeschichte des Neuen Testaments*, 1984; *Einführung in die Formgeschichte*, 1987, *Exegese des Neuen Testaments*, ³1992; *Bibelkunde des Neuen Testaments* ⁶1993; (on application and hermeneutics) *Hermeneutik des Neuen Testaments*, 1988. Other works include volumes of meditations, *Wie ein Vogel ist das Wort*, 1987; *Gottes einziger Ölbaum*, 1990, and *Historische Psychologie des Neuen Testaments*, 1991; *Exegese und Philosophie*, 1986.

Address: Brunnengasse 8/1, 69117 Heidelberg, Germany.

JOSÉ J. ALEMANY was born in Zaragoza, Spain, in 1937. He joined the Society of Jesus and was ordained priest in 1967. He has a first degree in philosophy and literature from the University of Barcelona, and a doctorate in theology from Innsbruck. He is Professor of Fundamental Theology and currently Dean of the Theology Faculty in the Pontifical

University of Comillas (Madrid). He is an associate of the Instituto Fe y Secularidad in Madrid and of the Centro de Estudios Ecuménicos y Orientales in Salamanca. His most recent book is *Las Iglesias cristianas entre la particularidad y la catolicidad* (1993).

Address: Universidad Pontificia Comillas, Facultad de Teologia, 28049 Madrid, Spain.

ANNE FORTIN-MELKEVIK was born in Quebec in 1957 and studied theology there. She gained a doctorate in religious anthropology and history of religions at the Sorbonne and a doctorate in theological science at the Institut Catholique de Paris in 1991. The title of her thesis was 'Towards a Rational Theory of Hermeneutics in Theology'. Since then she has been teaching fundamental theology at the Faculty of Theology of the Université Laval, Quebec. She has written a number of articles on ethics, modernity and postmodernity, which have appeared in *Studies in Religion/Sciences Religieuses*, *Le Supplément* and *Concilium*.

Address: Faculté de Théologie, Université Laval, Quebec, Canada G1K 7P4.

NORBERT METTE was born in Barkhausen/porta, Germany in 1946. After studying theology and sociology he gained a doctorate in theology, and since 1984 he has been Professor of Practical Theology at the University of Paderborn. He is married with three children, and is an Editorial Director of *Concilium*. He has written numerous works on pastoral theology and religious education, including: *Voraussetzungen christlicher Elementarerziehung*, Düsseldorf 1983; *Kirche auf dem Weg ins Jahr 2000* (with M Blasberg-Kuhnke), Düsseldorf 1986; *Gemeindepraxis in Grundbegriffen* (with C. Bäumler), Munich and Düsseldorf 1987; *Auf der Seite der Unterdrückten? Theologie der Befreiung im Kontext Europas* (ed. with P. Eicher), Düsseldorf 1989; *Der Pastorale Notstand* (with O. Fuchs), Düsseldorf 1992.

Address: Liebigweg 11a, D 48165 Münster, Germany.

Members of the Advisory Committee for Fundamental Theology

Directors

Claude Geffré OP	Paris	France
Werner Jeanrond	Dublin	Ireland

Members

José J. Alemany	Madrid	Spain
Edmund Arens	Frankfurt	Germany
Gregory Baum	Montreal	Canada
Luis Alberto de Boni OFM	Porto Alegre	Brazil
Maurice Boutin	Montreal	Canada
Rebecca Chopp	Chicago	USA
Anne Clifford	Pittsburgh	USA
Adela Cortina	Valencia	Spain
Richard Cote OMI	Ottawa	Canada
Antoine Delzant	Paris	France
José Fondevila SJ	Barcelona	Spain
Anne Fortin-Melkevik	Laval	Canada
Ottmar John	Ibbenbüren	Germany
Jean-Pierre Jossua	Paris	France
Werner Kroh	Münster	Germany
Pierre Gisel	Lausanne	Switzerland
Bernard Lauret	Paris	France
Johann Baptist Metz	Münster	Germany
Josef Meijer zu Schlochtern	Gelsenkirchen	Germany
Anand Nayak	Corminboeuf	Switzerland
Raimundo Panikkar	Barcelona	Spain
Manuel Reyes-Mate	Madrid	Spain
Heinz Robert Schlette	Bonn	Germany
Francis Schüssler Fiorenza	Cambridge, Mass	USA
Janet Martin Soskice	Cambridge	England
Christoph Theobald	Paris	France
John Edwin Thiel	Fairfield	USA
David Tracy	Chicago	USA

Directors/Counsellors

Jürgen Moltmann	Tübingen	Germany
Aloysius Pieris SJ	Gonawala-Kelaniya	Sri Lanka
James Provost	Washington, DC	USA
Edward Schillebeeckx	Nijmegen	The Netherlands
Christoph Theobald SJ	Paris	France
Miklós Tomka	Budapest	Hungary
David Tracy	Chicago, IL	USA
Marciano Vidal CSSR	Madrid	Spain
Knut Walf	Nijmegen	The Netherlands
Christos Yannaras	Athens	Greece

General Secretariat: Prins Bernardstraat 2, 6521 AB Nijmegen, The Netherlands
Manager: Mrs E. C. Duindam-Deckers.

Concilium Subscription Information - outside North America

Individual Annual Subscription (six issues): £30.00

Institution Annual Subscription (six issues): £40.00

Airmail subscriptions: add £10.00

Individual issues: £8.95 each

New subscribers please return this form:
for a two-year subscription, double the appropriate rate

(for individuals)	£30.00	(1/2 years)	. . . .
(for institutions)	£40.00	(1/2 years)	. . . .
Airmail postage outside Europe +£10.00		(1/2 years)	. . . .

Total . . . .

I wish to subscribe for one/two years as an individual/institution
(delete as appropriate)

Name/Institution . . . .

Address . . . .

. . . .

. . . .

I enclose a cheque for . . . . payable to SCM Press Ltd

Please charge my Access/Visa/Mastercard no. . . . .

Signature . . . . .Expiry Date . . . .

Please return this form to:
SCM PRESS LTD 26-30 Tottenham Road, London N1 4BZ